Superstar
in a HOUSEDRESS

Superstar

in a HOUSEDRESS

The Life and Legend of Jackie Curtis

Craig B. Highberger

Chamberlain Bros.
a member of Penguin Group (USA) Inc.
New York

CHAMBERLAIN BROS.
Published by the Penguin Group
Penguin Group (USA) Inc., 375 Hudson Street, New York, New York 10014, USA
Penguin Group (Canada), 10 Alcorn Avenue, Toronto, Ontario, Canada, M4V 3B2
(a division of Pearson Penguin Canada Inc.)
Penguin Books Ltd, 80 Strand, London WC2R 0RL, England
Penguin Ireland, 25 St Stephen's Green, Dublin 2, Ireland (a division of Penguin Books Ltd)
Penguin Group (Australia), 250 Camberwell Road, Camberwell, Victoria 3124, Australia
(a division of Pearson Australia Group Pty Ltd)
Penguin Books India Pvt Ltd, 11 Community Centre, Panchsheel Park, New Delhi–110 017, India
Penguin Group (NZ), cnr Airborne and Rosedale Roads, Albany, Auckland 1310, New Zealand
(a division of Pearson New Zealand Ltd)
Penguin Books (South Africa) (Pty) Ltd, 24 Sturdee Avenue, Rosebank, Johannesburg 2196, South Africa

Penguin Books Ltd, Registered Offices: 80 Strand, London WC2R 0RL, England

LIBRARY OF CONGRESS CATALOGING-IN-PUBLICATION DATA
Highberger, Craig B.
    Superstar in a housedress : the life and legend of Jackie Curtis / by Craig B. Highberger.
      p. cm.
    ISBN 1-59609-079-0
    1. Curtis, Jackie, 1947–1985.   2. Warhol, Andy, 1928–1987—Friends and associates.   3. Authors,
American—20th century—Biography.   4. Transvestites—United States—Biography.   5. Entertainers—
United States—Biography.   6. Actors—United States—Biography.   I. Title.
PS3553.U69425Z69   2005   2005041257
818'.5409—dc22
[B]

Printed in the United States of America
1   3   5   7   9   10   8   6   4   2

Book design by Jaime Putorti

For Jackie, whom I adored, and especially for my life partner, Andy—and all the friends, both old and new, who have shared their private memories of Curtis

Jackie Curtis posing in suburban Pittsburgh during a visit to the author, July 1983. (Photo by Craig Highberger)

I want to hit the heights. I want to be a Broadway star. I don't want to be just a cheap lady of the chorus who is always yearning for a star on the door and a dressing room full of red roses! I feel like a superstar in a housedress, because all I really care about is my work.

I'm not a boy, not a girl, not a faggot, not a drag queen, not a transsexual—I'm just me, Jackie.

—Jackie Curtis

CONTENTS

FOREWORD

In early 2000, when Craig Highberger called to tell me he was making a feature-length biographical documentary on Jackie Curtis's life, it was as if eighteen years of sadness and grief had lifted right out of my body. Since the day Curtis died, all of his belongings, photographs, scrapbooks, and diaries remained boxed up and dormant in my closet, waiting for an angel to assemble the detritus of his life into both a spectacular film documentary and a written remembrance. No more perfect an angel than Highberger himself.

A longtime friend of Curtis's, Craig had documented his life since being in NYU's film school back in the seventies. Jackie was in the prime of his career, and Craig, with true foresight, started his camera rolling, creating what would become major "drag world" historical footage. This footage was the foundation of *Superstar,* and it was instrumental in the revival of Curtis's *Glamour, Glory, and Gold* almost thirty years later.

On behalf of our family and myself, I sincerely thank Craig Highberger and his partner, Andy, for their exhaustive and loving dedication to Jackie Curtis's life. Their work has been creative, thoughtful, sensitive, and professional. They have brought the surviving friends, relatives, and colleagues of Curtis's together again, and have introduced his life and work to countless others all over the world. The spirit of God and love certainly reign supreme in the heart of Craig Highberger.

—In loving memory of my cousin and Godfather Curtis,
Joe Preston, Executor of the Estate of Jackie Curtis
July 2004

A collect for Jackie Curtis, delivered by the Reverend Timothy Holder, Jackie Curtis's brother, on the occasion of the premiere of *Superstar in a Housedress*, New York City, May 5, 2004.

Let us pray.

O God, Creator, Redeemer and Sustainer, Mother and Father of all the Lower East Side, of Slugger Ann, Jackie, La Mama, Andy, and us all, bless, we pray, our "Superstar in a Housedress," dazzling for all eternity in angel gown and heavenly glitter. Thank you for blessing the heart and hands of Craig Highberger in the creation of this film, and bless this story of a child of your own making, Jackie Curtis, Superstar.

Bless all this night, especially in our city, those who create yet are given little; those who work day and night, those without employment; those who try to celebrate the life you have given yet live with addiction and pain. Give us all, we pray, the courage and love you gave Jackie, the courage and love to be who we are, "not boy, not girl," just each your beautiful and distinct child, your creation, your love. Keep us, we ask, with Jackie and all your Stars, in your never ending "Glamour, Glory, and Gold.'"

Amen.

INTRODUCTION

John Holder, Jr., was born in New York City on February 19, 1947. He died of a drug overdose on May 15, 1985, at the age of thirty-eight. In his short life, under the name he chose for himself—Jackie Curtis—he became an actor, a singer, a published poet, a playwright, a director, and, most famously, a Warhol Superstar.

His father, John B. Holder, was a Veterans Administration worker, and his mother, Jean Uglialoro, was a certified public accountant. They met at a New York City dance hall where Jean, her sister, Josie, and her mother, Slugger Ann, worked as taxi dancers—women who would dance with men for a "fare." Jean married John and soon became pregnant. After John Jr.'s birth, the three moved to Holder's hometown, Stony Creek, Tennessee. But Jean missed the big city and could not adjust to life in a small town environment. Unfortunately, John had no desire to return to New York, so the couple split up. Jean moved back to the city with her infant.

John Jr. was a loner as an adolescent and spent as much time as possible at the movies. Too, Carol Burnett was starring in *Once Upon a Mattress* off-Broadway just across the street from where he lived, and her performance was a revelation. He decided then to change his name to Jackie Curtis and become an actor.

Jackie Curtis first appeared on stage at the age of seventeen, at La Mama Experimental Theater Club, in Tom Eyen's *Miss Nefertiti Regrets* (1965). He played Ptolemy but was upset because his costar

Bette Midler played Miss Nefertiti, the better role. This is when he began dressing in drag, and when he first met Andy Warhol and Paul Morrissey, who cast him as a female in their films *Flesh* and *Women in Revolt*. Jackie himself began writing plays that lampooned sexuality and made fun of social conventions, including *Glamour, Glory, and Gold* (1967), which starred Candy Darling and Robert De Niro, in his first stage role, and *Americka Cleopatra* (1972), in which costar Harvey Fierstein played Jackie's mother. Jackie's plays *Heaven Grand in Amber Orbit*, produced by John Vaccaro's Play-House of the Ridiculous in 1970, and *Vain Victory: The Vicissitudes of the Damned* (1971) were both huge hits. The *New York Times*, *Newsweek*, and the *Village Voice* described these avant-garde plays as "ridiculous," "outrageous," "bizarre," and "disorienting," but they sold out for months nonetheless.

Jackie Curtis spent years both living and performing in his unique style of drag, which usually included a wig, foundation makeup with some glitter around the eyes, and a 1930s gown held together with safety pins. Depending upon his mood, he would sometimes dress as a man and affect a James Dean persona. You never knew if he would show up as a girl or as a boy. But Curtis created more than just plays, poetry, and entertainment; he exuded an amazing energetic aura of boundless creativity that drew others to him like moths to a flame. Jackie was an artist whose greatest masterpiece was his own persona, which constantly amused and astonished those in his magical orbit.

I began the work of documenting Jackie Curtis's life and work more than thirty years ago. I started by videotaping Curtis starring in *Glamour, Glory, and Gold* in the summer of 1974. More recently, I spent nearly four years contacting surviving friends and colleagues of Jackie's, eventually interviewing more than thirty of them for my award-winning, feature-length biographical documentary *Superstar in a Housedress: The Life and Legend of Jackie Cur-*

tis. This book includes excerpts from all of those interviews, plus many wonderful stories that could not be included because of limitations of the documentary form. It also includes selections from many interviews I conducted after finishing the film, as well as poetry, scenes from plays, and excerpts from personal letters, journals, and "trip books"—works written under the influence of amphetamine. I am deeply honored by everyone who shared private memories of and tributes to Jackie Curtis with me. Those who had the good fortune to know him will always sorely miss his unique talents and spirit.

—Craig Highberger
July 2004

TIMELINE OF JACKIE CURTIS'S LIFE

FEBRUARY 19, 1947: John Holder, Jr., is born in New York City. His father, John Holder, Sr., moves his wife, Jenevive (Jean) Uglialoro Holder, and infant son to his hometown, Stony Creek, Tennessee.

SEPTEMBER 1947: Jean cannot adjust to life in Tennessee and seeks a separation from John. She returns to New York with John Jr., moves in with her mother, Anna Marino Uglialoro, and returns to work in the dance halls, as she did before she was married. Grandmother Uglialoro, known as "Slugger Ann," takes over primary responsibility for raising her grandson.

1948: John and Jenevive are divorced.

MID-1950S: Grandmother Uglialoro, who had managed a speakeasy during Prohibition, and worked in bars, dance halls, and strip clubs all her life, opens Slugger Ann's Bar on Second Avenue at Twelfth Street, in New York City. She marries Joe (Chinky) Verra.

JANUARY 30, 1955: Timothy Scott Holder, John Jr.'s half brother, is born in Tennessee.

MARCH 1, 1959: John Jr.'s aunt, Josephine Preston, gives birth to Joseph (Joey) Preston.

MAY 11, 1959: *Once Upon a Mattress* opens at the Phoenix Theater, with Carol Burnett playing the part of Princess Winnifred. Twelve-year-old John Jr. becomes a huge fan. Decades later, he will tell Michael Musto that Burnett is his "spiritual godmother," and that her performance is what guided him to a life in the theater.

1962: John Jr. enrolls in the High School of Art and Design in New York City.

1963: Young Susana Ventura, later known as "Penny Arcade," and John Jr. become inseparable friends. Behind closed doors at Susana's parents' apartment, she dresses him in drag for the first time.

1965: John Jr. changes his name to Jackie Curtis. He meets director Ron Link, and finishes writing his first play, *Glamour, Glory, and Gold*, soon after graduating from high school.

DECEMBER 1, 1965: Jackie, age seventeen, appears on stage for the first time at La Mama Experimental Theater Club in Tom Eyen's *Miss Nefertiti Regrets*.

MARCH 30, 1966: Jackie meets drag queen Holly Woodlawn.

SPRING 1966: Candy Darling, another drag queen, and Holly find a doctor who provides them with oral and injectable female hormones. Both are thrilled with the changes—softer skin, higher voices, diminishing facial hair, and breast development. Jackie experiments with female hormones for the first time.

HALLOWEEN 1966: Jackie attends a party in full drag for the first time, with Candy Darling and Holly Woodlawn.

AUGUST 1967: Jackie and Candy Darling meet Andy Warhol while walking through Greenwich Village.

SEPTEMBER 1967: *Glamour, Glory, and Gold: The Life and Legend of Nola Noonan, Goddess and Star* premieres at Bastiano's Theater on Waverly Place in New York City. Directed by Ron Link, the cast features Melba LaRose, Jr., as "Nola Noonan." Jackie and Candy Darling play female roles. Andy Warhol attends, and provides Jackie with a quote for publicity: "For the first time, I wasn't bored." The reviews are good, and the play runs for six months.

MARCH 28, 1968: *Lucky Wonderful,* a musical loosely based on the escapades and loves of asbestos heir Tommy Manville, premieres at the Playwrights Workshop. The book is by Jackie, with music and lyrics by Paul Serrato. Jackie plays the starring role, and the cast includes Melba La Rose, Jr., Pamela Galloway, Mary Carter, Roz Kelly, Harry York, Ronald Towe, and Rick Dolph. It receives mixed reviews.

MAY 1968: The second production of Jackie's *Glamour, Glory, and Gold* opens, this time with Paula Shaw playing Nola Noonan. In the cast, a young newcomer, Robert De Niro, plays four different men's roles. He receives a rave review in the *Village Voice*. Candy Darling and Jackie play assorted female roles.

JUNE 3, 1968: Valerie Solanas bursts into Andy Warhol's "Factory" and shoots him. The single bullet she fires pierces Warhol's left lung, spleen, stomach, liver, esophagus, and finally right lung. He barely survives hours of emergency surgery. Later that evening, Valerie turns herself in to a rookie traffic officer in Times Square, retrieving a .32 automatic and a .22 pistol from her raincoat pockets and handing them to him. She states that she shot Warhol because "he controlled my life."

SUMMER 1968: Paul Morrissey directs Andy Warhol's *Flesh* on weekends while Warhol recuperates from his gunshot wounds. The entire production costs approximately $1,500. Warhol never actually attends any of the filming.

SEPTEMBER 1968: *Flesh*, the film debut of Jackie Curtis and Candy Darling, opens at the Garrick Theater. It gets mixed reviews but draws huge crowds, and after playing at the Garrick for seven months, it moves to the 55th Street Playhouse in May 1969. The average gross is $2,000 per week.

DECEMBER 1968: Jackie has "Andy" tattooed on his left shoulder as a tribute to Warhol.

JUNE 1969: John Vaccaro, founder of the Play-House of the Ridiculous, casts Jackie in the chorus of *Cockstrong*.

JULY 21, 1969: Jackie plans to marry Eric Emerson on the rooftop terrace of an apartment building at 211 East Eleventh Street. Press and underground stars and artists are in attendance, including Andy Warhol, Larry Ray, Melba LaRose, Jr., Anthony J. Ingrassia, and Ruby Lynn Reyner. Emerson fails to appear. A porno producer performs the ceremony anyway, with a stand-in groom.

AUGUST 1969: John Vaccaro begins rehearsals for Jackie's play *Heaven Grand in Amber Orbit*. He and Jackie argue over the direction of the production. In the end, Vaccaro has his way and turns the play into a musical.

SEPTEMBER 1969: *Heaven Grand in Amber Orbit* premieres at Vaccaro's Play-House of the Ridiculous, a small funeral-home-turned-theater on Forty-third Street. It is a huge hit, and Vaccaro enjoys high praise for his direction. Jackie and Vaccaro's conflicts escalate, however, and he fires Jackie. Ruby Lynn Reyner takes over the lead role.

FEBRUARY 24, 1970: *Heaven Grand in Amber Orbit* opens at La Mama.

MARCH 1970: Paul Morrissey begins filming Jackie, Holly Woodlawn, and Candy Darling in a film that would ultimately be titled *Women in Revolt*.

MAY 6, 1970: Jackie's play *Femme Fatale: The Three Faces of Gloria* premieres at La Mama. Scripted by Jackie and directed by Anthony J. Ingrassia, the cast includes Penny Arcade, Patti Smith, Mary Waronov, and Wayne County. It receives mixed reviews.

JUNE 1970: Andy Warhol's film *Trash* opens.

JUNE 6, 1970: Jackie Curtis divorces Eric Emerson.

JULY 1970: Yugoslavian director Dusan Makavejev shoots scenes with Jackie for *WR: Mysteries of the Organism*. The X-rated film explores theories of sexuality, and argues that Stalinism is a form of Freudian sexual repression. It features scenes of Jackie talking about his first sexual experience with a man.

SEPTEMBER 1970: Portraitist Alice Neel paints Jackie and Rita Redd. The oil painting is one of her earliest of a gay couple.

OCTOBER 1970: Jackie, Candy Darling, and Paul Ambrose audition in drag for the Broadway musical revival of *No, No, Nanette*, but none of them make the cast.

OCTOBER 28, 1970: Jackie Curtis marries Archie Dukeshire.

DECEMBER 1970: Rehearsals begin for Jackie's *Vain Victory: The Vicissitudes of the Damned*, at La Mama in the East Village.

APRIL 17, 1971: Jackie Curtis divorces Archie Dukeshire.

MAY 26, 1971: *Vain Victory* premieres at La Mama, with Jackie directing the production. Cast members include Candy Darling (who is eventually replaced by Holly Woodlawn), Paul Ambrose, Eric Emerson, Agosto Machado, Styles Caldwell, Ondine, Dorrian Gray, Clarice Rivers, and Mario Montez.

JUNE 1971: Jackie Curtis and Candy Darling are guests on Joe Franklin's *Down Memory Lane* television show, to promote *Vain Victory*.

AUGUST 1971: *Vain Victory* moves to the Workshop of the Player's Art (WPA) at 333 Bowery on the Lower East Side.

NOVEMBER 7, 1971: *Vain Victory* closes after a successful run of sixty-six performances.

NOVEMBER 12, 1971: *Women in Revolt* premieres under its first title, *Sex*, at the first Los Angeles Filmex film festival in California.

NOVEMBER 27, 1971: Jackie Curtis marries Hunter Cayce.

DECEMBER 17, 1971: *Women in Revolt* theatrically opens at the Cinema Theater in Los Angeles, retitled *Andy Warhol's Women*.

JANUARY 5, 1972: Jackie Curtis divorces Hunter Cayce.

FEBRUARY 14, 1972: Jackie Curtis marries Hiram Keller.

FEBRUARY 16, 1972: *Women in Revolt* premieres at the Cine Malibu in New York City.

MAY 1972: Jackie's play *Americka Cleopatra* premieres at the WPA, under the direction of Harvey Tavel. Jackie plays the lead, Harvey Fierstein plays his mother, "Incredibe," Alexis del Lago appears as Charmin Gale, and Agosto Machado plays Lady Iras. The reviews are mixed.

AUGUST 1972: Alice Neel paints *Jackie Curtis as a Boy*. It depicts him seated in her studio, wearing blue jeans, a baseball jersey, and sporting prominent five o'clock shadow.

NOVEMBER 1972: Lou Reed's "Walk on the Wild Side" is released both as a single and on his album *Transformer*, with lyrics immortalizing Jackie Curtis, Holly Woodlawn, Candy Darling, and Joe Dallesandro. It quickly rockets to number one, and some radio stations in the United States unwittingly air the unedited LP version, which includes lyrics about Candy "giving head."

DECEMBER 1972: Andy Warhol asks Jackie, Candy, and Holly what they would like for Christmas. Candy asks for a bottle of Chanel No. 5, Holly asks for a dress, and Jackie asks for a color television. Warhol grants all three requests.

MARCH 1, 1973: Jackie Curtis divorces Hiram Keller.

JUNE 9, 1973: Jackie Curtis marries Lance Loud.

SEPTEMBER 1973: Episode two of the groundbreaking documentary series about the Loud family, *An American Family*, airs on PBS. Filmed in 1971, it includes Lance Loud taking his mother Pat to see Jackie starring in *Vain Victory* at La Mama.

FALL 1973: Candy Darling is diagnosed with a rare form of leukemia, believed to be induced by the many illegal hormones she had injested over the years.

MARCH 21, 1974: Candy Darling dies of leukemia at the age of twenty-five at Columbus Hospital, a few blocks from Andy Warhol's Factory. Warhol pays for a funeral at Frank Campbell's uptown. Attendees include Jackie, Peter Allen, Paul Ambrose, Pat Ast, Tally Brown, Eric Emerson, Maxime de la Falaise, Victor Hugo, Sylvia Miles, and Paul Morrissey. Warhol does not attend. During the service, Candy's real gender and real name, James Lawrence Slattery, are not mentioned. A beautiful good-bye note written by Candy is read aloud, which includes the line: "I would like to say good-bye to Jackie Curtis, I think you're fabulous," causing Curtis to burst into tears.

MARCH 22, 1974: A revival of *Glamour, Glory, and Gold*, directed by Ron Link, opens at the Fortune Theater the night after Candy Darling's death. As the curtain goes up, Link walks onto the darkened stage and asks for a moment of silence in memory of Candy Darling, and then, on behalf of Jackie Curtis, dedicates the performance to her.

MAY 31–JUNE 8, 1974: Jackie and Holly Woodlawn appear together in "Cabaret in the Sky: An Evening with Holly Woodlawn and Jackie Curtis" at the New York Cultural Center. The show is a smash hit.

MAY 1975: Eric Emerson is found dead near the West Side Highway at the age of thirty-one. Although officially the cause of death is listed a hit-and-run, it is rumored that he overdosed and that his body was dumped there.

SPRING 1975: Jackie Curtis graduates from Hunter College, although not confirmed officially, and no diploma has ever been found; it was published in his obituary.

MAY 1975: Jackie reads in *Variety* that *James Dean: The Legend*, a made-for-TV biography, has been green-lighted for production. He travels to Hollywood to audition for the lead. Stephen McHattie is ultimately cast in the role.

SUMMER 1975: Jackie returns to drag, and plays a drag queen in an episode of Valerie Harper's television series *Rhoda*.

AUGUST 7, 1975: Jackie Curtis divorces Lance Loud.

JULY 1976: Jackie returns to New York City. Gossip columnists print photos of a very masculine Jackie with a crew cut, as well as rumors of his romantic involvement with Sandy Dennis. He tells one interviewer: "I want to be a boy now. Maybe I'll marry Sandy Dennis. Sandy has 28 cats—she has a dog, she could add me."

SEPTEMBER 23, 1976: A revival of *Heaven Grand in Amber Orbit* opens at La Mama, directed by John Vaccaro.

DECEMBER 24, 1976: Jackie Curtis marries Peter Groby.

MAY 1977: Jackie and Holly Woodlawn headline their separate cabaret acts at fashionable New York nightspots, including Reno Sweeney's.

JUNE 1977: Jackie becomes frustrated with life in New York and impulsively moves to Elisabethton, Tennessee, to try living with his father, stepmother, and half brother Tim.

SEPTEMBER 1977: Jackie goes to Los Angeles and stays with friends while trying to land parts in films or television.

JANUARY 1978: Jackie returns to New York City, moving back in with his grandmother Slugger Ann.

MAY 14, 1978: Jackie Curtis divorces Peter Groby.

AUGUST 15, 1978: Jackie's mother, whose full name was now Jenevive Uglialoro Holder Tarsio, dies of cervical cancer.

AUGUST 1979: *The Unmuzzled Ox: The Poets' Encyclopedia* is published. It includes "B-Girls," a poem by Jackie Curtis.

OCTOBER AND NOVEMBER 1979: Jackie returns to drag and performs Friday- and Saturday-night shows at Slugger Ann's. Jackie, wearing Slugger's wedding dress, sings an eclectic mix of songs, including "Everyone's Going to the Moon," "I Enjoy Being a Girl," and "A Star Is (Still) Born."

SPRING 1980: Jackie plays Mrs. X in Nick Markovich's play *Tyrone X.*

JULY 4, 1980: Jackie's grandmother Slugger Ann, Anna Marino Uglialoro Verra, dies of blood disease.

JULY 23, 1980: Jackie Curtis marries Kevin McPhee.

SEPTEMBER 14, 1981: Jackie Curtis divorces Kevin McPhee.

JUNE 1983: Jackie spends part of the summer in Pittsburgh, Pennsylvania, with Craig Highberger. They videotape performances of five of Jackie's poems, including "B-Girls," and shoot rolls of photographs.

APRIL 21, 1983: *I Died Yesterday*, a play by Nick Markovich, premieres at La Mama, starring Jackie as Frances Farmer. The show receives favorable reviews. The cast includes Penny Arcade, Peter Groby, Rita Redd, and Styles Caldwell. Jackie's cousin Joey Preston begins working as stage manager and assistant to Jackie.

WINTER 1983: Penny Arcade helps Jackie stop drinking by spending every night with him for months.

MARCH 1984: Jackie videotapes a pilot for *Moral Heights*, a gay television soap opera he scripted based on characters from *Breakfast at Tiffany's* and other movies. It is never telecast.

MAY 26, 1984: Jackie's final wedding takes place at No. 1 Fifth Avenue. The groom is Gary Majchrzak, and Andy Warhol's art dealer, Leo Castelli, gives Jackie away. Artist Larry Rivers and his jazz band provide music. After the ceremony, Jackie holds up an astrological chart and explains that his staged weddings had come full circle, and that this was to be the final one. Attendees include Andy Warhol, Jean-Michel Basquiat, and Melba LaRose, Jr..

SUMMER AND FALL 1984: Jackie's friend Gomadi begins supplying Jackie and Margo Howard-Howard with heroin. Jackie overdoses, but Margo revives him. The injection site becomes infected and Jackie is hospitalized at St. Vincent's Hospital in the West Village for nearly a month.

NOVEMBER 1984: Rehearsals begin for *Champagne*, Jackie's final play, at La Mama.

JANUARY 3, 1985: *Champagne* opens at La Mama, with Jackie playing the lead character, Piper Heidsieck. Reviews are mixed.

MARCH 1985: Jackie stops using drugs. He changes his name to Shannon Montgomery, and begins attending acting classes at the HB Studio. He starts auditioning for male roles in New York City–based theatrical productions and soap operas.

MAY 15, 1985: Jackie Curtis dies of an accidental heroin overdose at the age of thirty-eight. His wake is held at the Andrett Funeral Home on Second Avenue and Twenty-first Street, with the funeral mass at St. Ann's Church. Jackie is laid out in his coffin as a man, with his hair slicked back, wearing a dark suit with a big white flower pinned to the lapel. Photographs of him in drag are arranged on poster-board displays, and a plaque reading "John Holder, a.k.a. Jackie Curtis" is placed inside the coffin. Paul Morrissey and Andy Warhol send flowers but do not attend.

CHAPTER 1

Youth

Gretchen Berg photographed Jackie Curtis in 1966 when he was just nineteen years old. She remembers: "There was something tragic and very sad in his eyes, even when he smiled." (Photo by Gretchen Berg)

Gretchen Berg

It was the hot summer of 1966, America was getting involved with Vietnam, people were marching in the streets, there was a lot of marijuana smoke in the air, like the smell of flowers, and I went up to East Forty-seventh Street, to the studio, the "Factory," of Andy Warhol. I did an interview with him, and I also took photographs. And when I finished, this young kid walked up to me. He was very tall. He had a football player's physique, and he said, "Hello, my name is Jackie. I need some pictures for my portfolio, would you take some pictures of me?" I introduced myself, and he said, "I talked to Gerard [Malanga], I know all about you. You know, Andy wants me to star in a film about his life, I'm going to play Andy as a boy."

So the next day or two, we went out together in the East Village and took a lot of photographs. Jackie Curtis was like some flowers—they're very bright and happy during the day, but at dusk he started to get more and more melancholy. Some people are like that; they take on the coloring, the mood of the night. Jackie seemed to be more of a night creature in many ways. And when the moodiness hit him, that's when I took my very best pictures of him. There was something tragic and very sad in his eyes, even when he smiled. He had the same sadness that you see in some Gypsy children—mirth without happiness. There seemed to be a definite tragic air about him, as if he were conscious of his destiny. Jackie was all alone in the world. His parents had divorced and had started other families. He was living with his grandmother over a bar called Slugger Ann's on Twelfth Street and Second Avenue. He was very conscious of the fact that he had to make his own way in the world.

Reverend Tim Holder

I'm Jackie Curtis's brother. Jackie used to talk about having family in Buladine, Tennessee. He was a member of the Buladine Citizen's Club, which he joined one summer he spent there with us. Dad could not live in the big city, so the family moved to Tennessee. Jackie's mother could not live in Tennessee, which meant that they could not be together. So they divorced, and Jackie went with his mother to live in New York.

Jackie

I used to have a recurring dream when I was a child. I dreamed that I was in a small house, a small space, and I was just too big. It was nightmarish, and I was just trying to get out of there. I was a child of the Lower East Side, the ghetto. Trying to escape, I tried everything. I tried to be funny, I tried to sing, I shined shoes, I opened up cab doors, and I met famous stars. I ran an elevator at the Ziegfeld Theater, I was an usher, and I sold lemonade and chocolate and checked hats and coats. I went to the High School of Art and Design.... I wanted to go to Performing Arts [high school], I really did. But my mother said if I went to Performing Arts, I'd only be an actor. And if I was only an actor, what would happen during those times when I didn't get a job? She wanted me to have something to fall back on. So I went to Art and Design, but I didn't pay too much attention to art. [However,] I fared very well. I remember one teacher that taught American History. He really liked me. There was this test about the American Revolution and the war. And the Tories and the Whigs, and Betsy Ross and her little mousy friend, Molly Pitcher, who helped her sew the flag. And there was an essay question, "Why did these men win the war?," and I answered because these men fought very hard. They got up in the morning. They made each other coffee. They patted each other on the back, they read each other letters, and they said we've got to go out there and get the enemy. Want to get them? No, we'll get them tomorrow. Today, let's just scare them. What will our mothers say if we lose the war? What will our wives and children say? What are we going to do about our oak paneling, and the mahogany on the door? How are we ever going to have teas again? And what about the fine old lace? And this teacher just liked the attitude. I had a very strong sense of America and history. I still do. I always mention Amelia Earhart luggage in every play I write.

Styles Caldwell

Jackie came from a very colorful background. His grandmother was very nice, but she was a very tough lady too—she had to be, she ran a bar in a very rough working-class neighborhood. I mean, there were prostitutes who hung out at Slugger Ann's bar, and there was a whorehouse right upstairs at one point. For years, there was a numbers racket going on out of the place too. Jackie told me all of this. In the early 1930s, during Prohibition, his grandmother Slugger Ann ran a New York speakeasy, so you can imagine there was probably Sicilian Mafia involvement from way back.

Jackie had a couple of uncles who had been Marines in World War II. They were Slugger Ann's sons, Jack and Tony. Uncle Jackie, he was really nice, but he had shell shock, or some nervous or psychological disorder, from the horrible experiences he had in the war. Uncle Tony was not nice at all. He was really macho and bullheaded, and when Jackie started running around in a dress Uncle Tony chased him around the city with a gun. He wanted to beat Jackie up because he said he was a disgrace to the family name. For years, Jackie had to always watch out for him, so he wouldn't go into the parts of the city where Uncle Tony worked or hung out. It sounds unbelievable, but it's true. Jackie talked about it on the *David Susskind Show* in the early seventies, and that was when the whole family was still alive, and they were all watching it at Slugger Ann's bar, so you know it's true. When Uncle Tony died of a heart attack, in his car with his girlfriend, everybody was very relieved.

Lily Tomlin

I relate to Jackie because of my own background in Detroit. I lived in a working-class neighborhood that was very mixed racially and ethnically. I grew up living in a very old apartment house that was filled with all kinds of people. And I can imagine what it was like for Jackie hanging out at Slugger Ann's when he was young. My dad was also a big drinker and a gambler, and I went to all the bars and the bookie joints with him. And I was just kind of in love with everybody, and all the different classes and education levels and politics and all I ever really saw was how alike they were—how elevated and grand they could be and how low and base they could be, at another time, each one of them. And I could imagine Jackie seeing people at Slugger Ann's through similar eyes.

On my Edith Ann album, I have Edith yelling into Parr's bar, "Hey Ed, is my dad in there?" And we had a soundtrack of a bar, and a gregarious old woman talking in the background, "Hey, what're ya doin' Ed?"—you hear pool cues cracking and balls breaking, and it probably was just like Slugger Ann's.

Sasha McCaffrey

Jackie Curtis told me that her grandmother Slugger Ann had been a burlesque queen, a vaudeville stripper. She was also the mistress of former New York Mayor Jimmy Walker. Walker bought her the Slugger Annie's bar so she could retire from stripping. She encouraged Jackie to get into show business. Slugger had enormous breasts and sometimes would wear this low-cut dress. Believe it or not, she would occasionally come into the bar with her seven tiny Chihuahuas inside her dress. She would have them perched on top of her once-voluptuous breasts, hanging out of the top of her dress for laughs! Everyone in the bar would just flip out. Just imagine these seven little glaring doggies yipping and yapping like the Medusa's head of snakes. . . . A very strange woman, Slugger Annie.

Jackie

One of the greatest things my grandmother ever told me was: "Don't cut your hair—your ears will show. Don't ever let anybody tell you you're handsome—because you're too tall, gaunt, awkward, and scary-looking. But you're lucky. Be nice but beware. Believe in yourself and everyone else will believe. I think it's fine to be considered strange because you're certain to be noticed. An individual is remembered."

Gretchen Berg

Jackie really wanted to break out and be on his own after high school, but he became frightened a lot. Life was very scary to him. Jackie tried living with friends many times during his life, but he always went back to Slugger Ann's. He never really had his own home. You need a place of your very own. You need a place where you can go and just shut the door and the whole world is outside. He didn't really have that. He didn't really have a father or mother in his life. He managed to bury that, but it came up later in his twenties and thirties in alcohol and drug abuse.

He once confided to me that he was still a virgin at eighteen, and that he was scared to have sex with anybody. He said that when he was told "the facts," as he called them, he said to the other kids, without thinking, "My mother and father never did that!," and he was subjected to much merciless ragging. He almost never mentioned his family—I didn't even know he had a brother—and the only time he mentioned his mother was once when he spoke of leaving high school: "I knew my mother wouldn't have served another plate of food to me, so I got that high school diploma!"

Jackie once said to me, "Girls really have it good because they can dress in skirts or they can dress like a boy." He would often make statements that were really questions. It was really as if he was asking me, *Is this right? Should I think these things? Is it right to feel this way?* Jackie didn't have anyone to show him what a man is in this society. He didn't know if he should be straight, bisexual, or homosexual—it was all very confusing to him as an adolescent, and it wasn't something I could help him with.

Jackie

When I was a teenager, I sought out all the greats in the New York theater world and went to them as a student would go to a master, to learn and work. They recognized my talents, and they wanted to help me. But some of them were interested in helping me in other ways. Some of them were interested in special talents. If you get my meaning. They wanted to help me, all right. Help me into the bed. And I'd say, "No. I have to go home to my grandmother now." And it was true, it wasn't an alibi. I wanted to work with them, not sleep with them. I was brought up a good Italian Catholic girl by my mother, my aunt, and my grandmother.

Joey Preston

Curtis was one of my dearest family members. As early as I was doing my first communion, Curtis had been in drag the night before for the first time. He shocked my grandmother, my mother, and my aunt—needless to say. But the next morning, he was bright and early in St. Ann's Church, being my godfather.

My first memories of Curtis dressed in drag are when he came up to the house with Holly Woodlawn and Candy Darling. We lived in a railroad apartment, and I would sit in my room and the three of them would go back and forth from the bathroom fixing their makeup, with the feather boas, the glitter all over the place. I actually had no clue that this was Curtis dressed up as a woman. I'm ten years old, sitting on my bed, looking up at these tall drag queens with feather boas flying behind them; they're all looking at me as they're passing. It was quite a novelty for me. I knew the life way before I grew up.

Curtis was always at odds with our uncle Tony. The first time Uncle Tony saw him in drag, they had a few choice words, and Tony chased him out of the bar and right down Twelfth Street. Imagine Curtis with the feathers and the high heels running down the block with this angry macho street man chasing after him! Uncle Tony never caught up with him. Curtis was fast enough, thank God.

Gretchen Berg

Jackie actually did try to hold office jobs. He did try to have a straight life and earn some money so he wouldn't have his family supporting him. So he would go to a New York temp agency and they would send him to these clerical jobs. He would go in his peacoat with his shopping bag. He told me he was a great hit with a lot of the offices because, "Nobody reads an invoice like Jackie." He would deliver the mail and answer the phones. He told me that he looked at these jobs as if he had been given a part in a play or a movie, and said, "I did my best. I played my part. I was wonderful." However, one day he arrived at one of these jobs wearing a wig and a dress with sequins and delivered the mail in drag. That was the end of that job, and, after that, I don't think he spent much time in offices.

Reverend Tim Holder

As an adolescent, I came to question my brother's sexuality, wondering was Jackie gay, was he straight, was he transgendered? And, frankly, at first I was very ashamed that such a person was in my family.

Later, I myself addressed my own sexuality, having become not too many years ago the first openly gay priest in the diocese of Alabama. I look back in celebration of Jackie's life, and I remember one interview quote in particular. Jackie told a persistent reporter, "I am not gay, I am not straight, I am just me, Jackie." That was a real proclamation of liberation: Do not label me, do not categorize me.

Jackie

My parents were divorced when I was a child. I was a Tennessee Baptist six months of the year and a New York Roman Catholic the rest of the year. And to go into what that would do to a child's mind, I'm still trying to figure it out. It was very hard to find myself as a boy. When I was an adolescent and went to the movies, I realized that I identified with the female characters. And then the lights would come up and I was attracted to people of the same sex. I don't think of myself as gay, although I do sleep exclusively with men. But sex is not my main goal either. Sexual relations don't play the largest part in my makeup. My makeup doesn't play the largest part either. Most drag queens stuff their brassieres, and pad their buns—I don't think I need that. My body is proportioned just the way it is supposed to be. Anything else would make me feel off balance. And already I'm disconnected enough.

Gretchen Berg

Jackie would come up to my hotel, the Wellington, at Seventh Avenue and Fifty-fifth Street, and we would hang out. In those days he always wore a peacoat, and carried a shopping bag full of magazines, records, and clippings—all kinds of interesting things. Jackie was starting his career, and he went to all the open-call auditions and met a lot of celebrities from the New York theater world. He told me he asked Edith Head to design him a tie clip, and asked Milton Berle to write material for him.

Jackie told me that he was fat and bullied as a child, but he developed a way of dealing with the bullies by cursing a blue streak at them. They reacted by saying, "What a dirty mouth he has, don't have anything to do with him." So he cursed and swore, and everybody kept away from him. Jackie grew into a very good-looking young man, but I could always see that tragic air about him.

We used to go down to Times Square, to Forty-second Street when it *was* Forty-second Street, not the very cleaned-up nice place it is today; it was really raunchy with lots of porno theaters and strip joints. We'd go to the movie theaters all day; there were dozens of them in those days, and some of them just ran old films. I remember watching Sam Fuller's *Pickup on South Street* with Jackie, which is a really rough film noir. He got very excited, and said to me, "This is the way adults really are, and if we get to know how they move, how they act, how they think, we'll really be able to handle them." So we stayed and watched it three times. You could do that on one admission in those days.

We were in the balcony of one of the fleabag theaters on Forty-second Street when a young man who was watching us came and sat in the row behind us. He leaned forward and said to Jackie, "Hi, cutie, I've got a word for you." Jackie replied, "I've got a word for you too, but there's a lady present." The young man stood up and walked away.

Jackie was always trying to come up with money to go to the movies. He fell asleep one night in the balcony and woke up to Judy Garland singing "The Trolley Song." Jackie told me one time he came home from a day at the movies and his grandmother was really angry and said, "What are we going to do with you, sitting in the movies all day long eating popcorn and candy, getting your head filled up with dreams?" But Jackie said, "Listen, I like dreams. They're better than what I'm getting."

Ellen Stewart

Jackie Curtis came to La Mama in 1965 in Tom Eyen's *Miss Nefertiti Regrets*. This was the play that Bette Midler first appeared in as well. She played Miss Nefertiti, and Jackie played Ptolemy, her brother. Jackie was in many other plays at La Mama as well. In 1970, he wrote and starred in *Heaven Grand in Amber Orbit*, and in 1971 he was in *Vain Victory*. Jackie wrote the show, and Andy Warhol performed with Jackie here at La Mama.

Jackie was just a boy when he came to La Mama. And he lived with his grandmother Slugger Ann, who had a bar somewhere around Twelfth Street and Second Avenue. He was always extremely talented. In fact, I thought he was a genius. And he created many beautiful things. Jackie was a wonderful writer. And he said that being a drag queen brought him more fame, but he wished that his work as a playwright would establish him as a very great writer.

From the back of Jackie's 8 × 10 headshot, 1966:

JACKIE CURTIS
c/o Holder, 34 Orchard St., New York, 2, N.Y.

Age range: 14–21

Eyes: Expressive Brown

Hair: Light Brown

Height: 5' 11"
Weight: 150–155 lbs.

TRAINING

Henry Street Settlement (Dance & Drama), Gene Frankel Teenage Theater Workshop, Herbert Berghof Studios (Drama & Musical Comedy), High School of Art & Design (Theatre Arts & Creative Writing)

EXPERIENCE(S)
BROADWAY

FOXY with Bert Lahr, Larry Blyden & John Davidson
AMEN CORNER with Beah Richards & Frank Silvers
FUNNY GIRL with Barbra Streisand & Sydney Chaplin

OFF BROADWAY

SCROOGE (Peter Cratchitt & Fred) Actor's Playhouse
THIS WAS BURLESQUE (Candy Butcher) Casino East Theatre
HELLO, BURLESQUE (Candy Butcher & Bit Player) Gaiety Theatre
ALL WOMEN ARE ONE Theater Guild Production
THE PADLOCK (Ass't Stage Manager & Understudy) Theatre 62
APRIL MELODY (Tony) Theatre 62
A LADY NAMED JO (Ned Moffit) Toured N.Y. Public Schools
THE SWAGGERING SOLDIER (4 Slaves) Toured Libraries
ROOM Service (Messenger Boy) ELT Productions
MISS NEFERTITI REGRETS (Ptolemy II) Cafe La Mama Etc
CHARLIE, PUT YOUR DREAMS AWAY (Charlie) Cafe Cino

FILMS

LOVE REGAINED (Necrophiliac) Political Satire
ANDY WARHOL STORY (Andy Warhol) A Reynolds Wrap Prod.

LOVE ME, LOVE ME (Michael) 3 Star Films, Inc.

ANGEL RISE, ANGEL FALL (Rutherford Rembrandt) Independent Film

STOCK

BYE BYE BIRDIE (Hugo) Barter Theatre, Abingdon, Va.

TELEVISION

COMMUNITY DIALOGUE Channel 5

CANDID CAMERA Channel 2

WJHL (Bristol, Tenn). "Gospel Singing Jubilee"

WOR-TV, JOE FRANKLIN SHOW, "DOWN MEMORY LANE" Regular Guest

RADIO

WKCR-FM Scrooge Commercial

WNYE-FM Educational Broadcasting

WCAG-FM Jackie Curtis in Concert, plus Interview

WOR-AM & FM The Joe Franklin Show

NIGHTCLUBS

Gaslight, Sniffen Court Inn, Washington Square Room, Guys & Dolls, The Improvisation, Champagne Gallery, The No. 1 Fifth Avenue, and the River Room at the Hendric Hudson Hotel

MODELING

Underground Uplift Unlimited (Button Advt.), Christmas Card Sample, Upcoming Book: "The World of Andy Warhol," N.Y. Times Drama Section & Magazine Supplement, Rodale's Revue Magazine, Phoenix Theatre Publicity Stunts, Centaur Films, etc.

AUTO-BIO

I was born on an Ash Wednesday and am on the cusp of Pisces. In 1959 my friend Carol Burnett and I held a nation-wide publicized picket to save her show, "Once Upon a Mattress." I'm crazy for Spanish movies and soap operas, not that I understand a word that they say—they make nice faces. I always wanted to be a priest until I stopped watching Pat O'Brien movies. I was reviewed in the Village Voice, Daily News, and Variety—and I don't even have a stage mother. My Broadway credits are for apprenticing, sort of, better than doing stock in Tom's River. As for my speech pattern—that's all it is, and I comb my hair differently every day—it all depends upon my speech pattern. In school all the other kids had briefcases, attaché cases, and wore socks. I had a shopping bag. Listen, it lent a lot of character. I don't have a manager, but wouldn't deny anyone the position.

I know it's strange, but I'm not very fond of making the rounds and going to open-call auditions and seeing the same faces all the time. But for a while they were my only IN. Then I rebelled. One day at a very open call which required "pictures & resumes" they began handing out little white file cards demanding credits and such. So smart me opened my mouth: "But I brought a resume." But they insisted the card be filled out, so I wrote my name and address and then: "DOWN WITH WOOLWORTHS, SUPPORT THE UNDER-GROUND, SEND JOE PYNE TO COLLEGE, JEAN SHRIMP-TON IS REALLY A MAN, RIN TIN TIN IS A BITCH, YOU DON'T HAVE TO BE JEWISH TO LOVE ME, SEE RESUME FOR ADDITIONAL INFORMATION." So they HAD to look at my resume, and when they saw it they asked me, "How come you're not on TV, why are you here?" Anyway auditions and interviews most always leave me cold, UNLESS the people are nice. I like nice people, what else can I tell you?

I wasn't in "Who's Who" this year, that's 19 years now. Neither am I a beatnik. That's someone with long hair, crazy clothes, and strange ideas who needs a bath. I learned more at home than the average kid—for instance, my grandmother used to read palms, cards, tea leaves, bumps on heads, and hold seances. She taught me about reincarnation and astrology and gave me a book on superstitions. I was never allowed to bring a movie magazine into the house or anything like that, so at 16 I moved out and did everything from washing dishes to running elevators.

I'm from the Lower East Side, and don't know why four of us slept in one bed, we had four rooms and a couch. My childhood was frantic, like a Marx Bros. movie. My family was frantic, like the Marx Bros. I'm a loner. Independently independent. That's why I talk so much. I don't hang out anywhere. I hate hangouts! But I do haunt old bookshops and music stores, because you never know who or what you might find there. One of the best things my grandmother ever told me was: "You're a cusp, and don't forget it. C'mon, I gotta make a payment at the hock shop."

I love when people say I talk in the stream of consciousness— that means they're listening. I should be the first male to play PETER PAN, what can I say? (See my resume for additional information.)

Mom Eternal
A poem by Jackie Curtis

"It is the work one does himself,"
my Mother told me,
"and not what is handed to him ready made
that has the constructive power."
My Mother's name is Jenny and my Father's name is Johnny.

He was a Sailor
and she was a Singer.
Somewhere in the forties in New York,
a band started playing my Mother's favorite song . . .

You and your smile hold a strange INVITATION.

A song she'd heard in an MGM movie with the same name.
It starred Dorothy McGuire and Van Johnson.
My Mother had a voice with a subtle allure
beckoning beyond the veil of rhythm and blues
without leaving the rooms of heaven,
heralded by trumpets
while a band of angels proclaimed her presence . . .

Somehow it seems
we've shared our dreams
but where?
Indeed? Where?
It was The Great White Way and the journey toward
American Victory was everyone's aim without a doubt,
and without a song the day would never end
the War our country waged
like a temporary loneliness longing for the solitude
of United States of America's stationary
Orbit in Victory's Garden of Eden where
Ladies and Gentlemen all out were told,
"The choicest life is the life this Country Can Lead"

Time after time
in a room full of strangers
our love will bloom
suddenly you are there.

And there he was,
like an early morning glory
not at all cluttering up the vine . . .
On Liberty from the Navy (They Got the Gravy).
My Mother was first attracted to my Father
because he so resembled her favorite popular singer,
BING CROSBY.

Where ever I go
you're the glow of temptation.

He was a Southerner, a Rebel.
She was a Northerner, a Yankee.
Opposites attract.
They became close and in no time
were on their way to a Church Wedding–wedding.

Glancing my way
in the gray of the dawn
and always your smile
holds that strange INVITATION.

They were altar bound, within a warm Cathedral . . .
now "they" would march as "one."
Where they gathered in the sight of God, toward tomorrow,
they would become enveloped
in the only bonds they would leave the War with,
the bonds of Holy Matrimony.
To Love, Honor, Obey . . . to Cherish, in Sickness and in
*   Health.*

There they stood on this cynical threshold
this very certified sacrament having been "serialized"

by the second bona fide battle our country had begun.
This cliff-hanging Hero and his Lady Fair!
Love had been encouraged so as to have been "swept" clear . . .
*   across the country!!*
Meanwhile, Uncle Sam pointed imperiously at red-blooded
*   all-American Men*
indicating the now famous logo ("UNCLE SAM WANTS
*   YOU!").*
It even rhymes with, WORLD WAR TWO!!!
Never mind OVER THERE. My Mother to be,
her Husband to be, a Sailor once again
would casually be shipping out to sea for an anticipated Victory,
was presently taking the gigantic giant step into
*   MARRIAGE . . .*
by way of the stunning triumph of love, please, leave us not forget
one of the most oversold commodities of the forties . . . LOVE!

There they were, saying I Do
inside of a Roman CATHOLIC church
as if TIME! had been called.
He, off the ship on Liberty
being spent on the Northern shore with a Northern Sweetheart,
it was then that the clergyman pronounced them, quite
*   succinctly I am sure,*
MAN AND WIFE.
It is precisely at this moment we have been educated to learn
that said RING goes on THAT finger, preceding the very
*   exciting five words,*
"YOU MAY KISS THE BRIDE."
This is the kiss at this time that makes it all too clear
that time (I am referring to the War)
is running the ship, time is running a TIGHT SHIP,
as a matter of fact, they will set sails upon uncharted waters,

rushed is this my Mom's maiden voyage.
A romance so rude, whisked beyond white lace
becoming something even more vulgar than converted rice,
making haste for the heart's desire.
All of a simpering sudden, the simplest (!) and sacred most
    sensitive soul
to say nothing of the soul that is not half so inclined
and seems to have suffered the worst of disillusions
somewhere at sea, or dismantled perfection
from perhaps underneath the briny foam
atop the snowcapped waves
above the water which floats majestically
across seven of them,
seas, that is.

Vous comprendez?
(I am referring to the possible mythological
wherein we would have to go below where Poseidon
or perhaps Neptune would indeed intervene,
and only in MY CASE . . .
which as I heard it was the NEXT CASE!) . . .
And like the myths of this particular spirit,
likened earlier to that of Neptune (et al.)
conceiving of some silly Shanghai-honeymoon at sea,
mind you, in a bunk bed while the world raged on within the
    confines of War (II),
and don't tell me it was not confined . . .
on Land, in the Air, and at Sea along with such nautical
    appliances as:
Submarines, Periscopes (UP? did you say.).

Sailors at hand on Deck
while down below they are dealing the deadly torpedoes

along with the MayDays of the Day . . .
the Newlyweds (my incipient parents)
having to do severely WITHOUT our sweet, pristine world
where the wedding bells have been known to break out the news
from a way atop (and on high!)
that the New World's Man
(so you should now and forever know that I do not harbor
*   fantasies*
that my Pa is from another galaxy) and wife (this non-fantasy
*   includes my Ma!)*
serene in sumptuous Navy Splendor . . .
not a dream or whimsical make-believe
(don't you think I'd like to say to someone someday, SMILE!
*   I WAS BORN IN A HOSPITAL TOO!!).*
Even though (and here's the juicy part, people)
my Pa (Oh, my Pa Pa!) took a powder when I was two.
It is time for the throngs of relatives to be wishing them
(this goes for the Ma Ma! remember, as well . . . and may she
*   always be so!)*
well,
wishing well for them upon the r-r-r-road
they had so long ago embarked upon
beginning anew.
Alone
with the rest of their lives to make it all come true,
all right,
in loveland.

Jackie Curtis—the product of this love.

CHAPTER 2

Drag

Jackie Curtis in his "Barbra" wig at Max's Kansas City in 1973.
(Photo by Craig Highberger)

Alexis del Lago

Jackie was not a man, was not a woman—he was a way of life!

Penny Arcade

Curtis was one of the most magical people I've ever known, and I have known a lot of magical people. Curtis was like the Little Prince. That's who Jackie always reminded me of, because he had this incredible idealism, bravura, childish self-centeredness, and make-believe. Very few people maintain that spontaneity, that magic, that joy, that is every person's birthright. Very few people maintain that past the age of four, and Curtis was one of them. When you were in his presence you were in the presence of magic, and you knew it, and Jackie brought out your magic. But I think that was ultimately Jackie's downfall, because Jackie created this charmed world that he couldn't really come out of. He couldn't translate to the real world. He somehow was like a fish out of the ocean when he went into the real world.

When I met Jackie, I was heavily involved with the downtown drug scene, with the quintessential non-hippie, black, gay, criminal, junkie culture of downtown New York. I was shooting speed, I was shooting heroin, but I was mostly shooting speed. And I was whacked. I'm fifty-one now, so it's very hard for me to remember what I was like at eighteen, but I was a force of nature, let us say. That was at a time when most girls didn't consort with homosexuals or drag queens to the extent that I did. One of my big jokes is that in 1967, when I was seventeen, in Provincetown, it was widely believed that I was a sex change. . . . I'd be at a party in Provincetown in 1967—there'd be seventy-five gay men and me. And somebody would come up to me and say, "Is she real?," and I would go, "I did not spend seventy-five thousand dollars and three months in Casablanca to have you ask me if I am real!" So this rumor went around Boston, Ptown, and New York City for years and years that I was a sex change. . . .

I met Jackie as a boy, and zipped Jackie into his first dress. Actually, what drag queens and fag hags had in common was a great love for 1930s dresses. That's how we dressed. Curtis and I were always going looking for clothes at thrift shops. And Jackie started dressing like I did—in old-lady, lace-up shoes that had the big thick Cuban heel, thirties dresses, and black tights. The tights were always shredded 'cause we couldn't afford to buy them all the time, and we just didn't give a shit. And I always wore glitter at night, off stage.

When Curtis started doing drag, it was the over-the-top "Play-House of the Ridiculous" drag. . . . It was all about the big lips, big face, big eyes . . . and three pairs of false eyelashes. Jackie didn't have great hygiene, which is the mark of a real drag queen. Also, from doing so many drugs, he'd be up three straight days and nights, not changing that dress. There'd always be huge stains under the armpits. Remember, Jackie was Sicilian and Swedish, Jackie was six foot two, the body of a linebacker; Jackie had a very big frame. Jackie was not a delicate creature, and had the stubble, the glitter.

Jackie ushered in that period of not trying to look real. What everybody was going for in drag up until Jackie Curtis was realness. That was the criterion, how "real" did you look? Jackie could never hope to look real. It was never going to happen. So Jackie didn't use falsies. Jackie used his own eroticism.

Jackie

I transformed myself into Jackie Curtis because I wasn't getting enough attention. Nobody took me seriously when I went to auditions. But when I walk in as a girl, I am immediately accepted on a creative level. And that's true everywhere I go dressed as a girl. I actually put on a woman's dress, in one sense, to ward off evil spirits. Straight men found me threatening as a boy because they saw something they didn't like that scared them. When I dress as a girl, they can laugh at me if they want to, but they don't react with revulsion. They can come right up and feel completely comfortable interacting with me, as this hard hat did just the other day on Fifty-seventh Street. That kind of thing never happened when I was a boy. I felt completely invisible as a boy—like a ghost.

Steven Watson

According to Holly Woodlawn, Jackie, Holly, and Candy met at a party to watch the second Barbra Streisand special, *Color Me Barbra*, in the Greenwich Village apartment of someone who had a color television set. And Ron Link, who directed Jackie and lived with him, said that they always used to refer to each other as the trio from *How to Marry a Millionaire*, so it was Shotzie, Sugar, and Loco [Schatze, Pola, and Loco in the movie]. Candy had a kind of incredible, unreal glamour that was highly, highly worked at. Holly I think just had a lot of fun and enjoyment out of that unlikely moment of being a star in the Warhol movie *Trash*. But Jackie is for me at that moment especially important, because he is a star. He is also really questioning all sorts of things about sexuality and gender in a way that Candy's not questioning; Candy is wanting it.

Jackie is a girl, he's a boy—it's as if the idea of what your sex is is just a reflection of your feeling of your personality that day, and it changes, it's zigzag, it's a combination of Lucille Ball and a prize-fighter, and the references are all over the place. My guess is that Jackie had a huge IQ and probably severe cognitive ADD qualities, but he really focused into what he could do with that. It's the moment of gay liberation; Stonewall happens in June 1969, and less than a month later Jackie is having his wedding to Eric Emerson on this rooftop. As it turned out, Jackie didn't get married to Eric because he [Eric] did not show up, but Jackie took that all in stride and returned for the wedding reception at Max's Kansas City, where Eric worked, and he was totally amazed that everyone was paying so much attention to this, and Eric kind of sheepishly apologized to Jackie, and Jackie said, "Yes, I know, Eric. But I have a show to do now—my reception." That was so Jackie!

Jackie

It is very strange, but I only seem to get into trouble when I'm a boy. The worst was when the cops found a gun in my studio. It was inoperable, and a prop, but they arrested me anyway. I feel somehow the trouble I have as a boy compensates for the sensational time I have as one of the girls just sitting around.

You might think that being a gay boy would be more liberating—but for me it's not. Because I feel trapped as a boy. But you must understand that I don't feel like a woman trapped in the body of a male. Candy and Holly take female hormones and talk about having sex-change operations. That is not for me at all, because my body is my body, and my sex is my sex, and my ambiguity is my ambiguity. And I cling to that, fervently.

Lily Tomlin

Jackie tried not to look perfect—that whole thing of exaggerating the look and the torn stockings, it was just original and wonderful. Jackie didn't have a particularly feminine face, as Candy did, and that is what made his appearance more striking. Jackie and all of those wonderful artists at that time—and Jackie was really in the vanguard—they were outsiders, and they had that incredible sense of the absurdity of the whole culture. They're innovators, but, as Jane [Wagner] would say, they're also preservationists.

I got Candy Darling an audition at the Upstairs at the Downstairs. I thought Candy was so gorgeous, and I thought Rod Warren would cast her, and that he wouldn't even realize that Candy is a man dressing as a woman, but he didn't hire her. Later, in 1972, Candy was cast in Tennessee Williams's *Small Craft Warnings* off-Broadway. I heard that the male actors wouldn't allow her in their dressing room, and neither would the women, which was just terrible. After I got famous, on Rowan and Martin's *Laugh-In*, I always fantasized about doing a special with Candy and Jackie. Too bad I never did.

Lee Black Childers

Jackie was living with me on Thirteenth Street, and there was a very old lady named Rosie who lived right next door. She was a very sweet little old Italian widow, and we saw her all the time. And Rosie died. She was ninety. No sooner than they had the body out of the apartment, Jackie got out of our window, clinging to the building, shuffling along the ledge next to the fire escape, until she got to Rosie's window, which was open a bit. She got the window open with her foot and got inside. She stole all of Rosie's clothes, and then she shuffled back along the ledge with them, instead of just opening Rosie's door. And they were these black crepe dresses—she was an old Italian widow. If you look at pictures taken of Jackie at that time, she's wearing Rosie's clothes! But then, of course, unlike Rosie, she didn't bother to launder them. So they would become these really rotten garments falling apart on her.

Michael Arian

Jackie was always safety-pinned together, and had a way of using fabric or tablecloths or scarves in a way that most human beings would never consider using them. Jackie made the most elegant gown you've ever seen out of a big square tablecloth that had fringe on it.

Jackie either could make the room hate her, or love her. Jackie could entertain in the back room of Max's Kansas City like no one in history could—and it wasn't always by bringing unwanted attention to herself. Likely as not, it would be some methamphetamine-sparked run that would cause it—but Jackie could be very entertaining. She could also be very repellant at the same time. You could smell Jackie beneath the glamour.

Penny Arcade

Jackie and I had an enormous emotional, resonant, erotic relationship. I don't mean that it was sexual; it was energizing. We were an incredible team, and we patrolled. We were both from working-class immigrant Italian families, matriarchal families, and had a lot in common. We were both highly intelligent, belligerent, and lived in a fantasy world. And wanted to love the whole world. Both of us didn't take no for an answer. I joke with a lot of my gay male friends about their latent bisexuality. Jackie really didn't have any. Jackie was sort of asexual. Jackie's relationship was really with Jackie. Jackie wasn't really looking for a partner. He liked to go to a little park he called the Garden of Meditation and have anonymous sex with guys in the bushes or in the men's room. I think Jackie was a fairly promiscuous person who went for very long periods of time not having sex at all.

I remember being somewhere on Madison Avenue, uptown in the Eighties or Nineties, going to some rich people's party. Because, as Warhol superstars, we were invited to these parties with rich people, and the only thing that drag queens like better than drugs and booze is free food. The thing that really impresses drag queens is we'd go to these rich people's parties and there'd be all this food.

And we are all the way uptown and we've lost the address. And everybody is frantic we're going to miss the party. And I remember standing in the middle of Madison Avenue and saying, "We can't miss the fucking party; we *are* the party." And this was in 1967, and it wasn't an expression, a slogan, it was the reality, because straight rich people wanted wacky weirdos like us, and the entertainment didn't happen until the freaks arrived. Actually, at one point Warhol realized he had a good thing going, and that summer he announced he was starting this "rent a superstar" service for hostesses who wanted to liven up their boring Upper West Side cocktail parties.

Holly Woodlawn

I never had an apartment lease until I was maybe thirty. Who had to pay rent? Jackie, Candy, and I were the toasts of the town for years. Parties and places to go every night, different places to crash every day. We couch-surfed our way around Manhattan for years and years. We were professional houseguests.

Sasha McCaffrey

When I met Jackie Curtis, Holly Woodlawn, Candy Darling, and Taffy Tits, they had all just started living in drag twenty-four hours a day. Candy had crooked teeth and brown hair; Holly looked completely zany. I was looking for an apartment, and they had this little furnished, rent-controlled place. I had a job, so they encouraged me to move in with them. It turned out I was the only one working, so I was the one paying all the rent. They would go out all night, so I would get the bed. They would wait until morning, and then they would sleep when I got up to go to work.

They appeared to be women, so I really believed that they were women. For the first three months, I actually did not know that these were not real girls. I mean, I don't peek. One day, I did ask

Holly, "Why does Taffy wear all that heavy pancake makeup?" And Holly said, "Well, she's Sicilian. So like a lot of Sicilian women, she has to shave twice a day and wear lots of pancake makeup." It made sense to me. I was nineteen. What did I know about Sicilian women?

Holly would help get Candy ready for her date. Back in those days, in the sixties, you could still buy real nylon stockings with seams in them; they were very stylish, but they were also very expensive. I came home one night and Candy was standing on a chair in the kitchen. She was holding her skirt up, and Holly was standing behind her, with a black eyebrow pencil, slowly drawing a straight line down her naked leg, "Don't move, Candy." "You sure they're going to look like real nylon stockings?" Candy said. "They look so fabulous," Holly told her. "Just don't cross your legs, or you'll look like you're half black and half white. They won't know what you are." "Oh, they don't know what I am now," sighed Candy. "I'm Jeanne Eagels."

Taylor Mead

Holly Woodlawn and Jackie Curtis would wander all over Manhattan dressed in the most tasteless drag imaginable. It was obvious that they were male, not female. And they had these awful dresses; it looked like they were wearing carpets carved out like dresses. But I admired them tremendously; I thought, What nerve it must take to do that. And I always wanted to go out in drag as a nun or something, but I never had the nerve to do it.

Mona Robson

One afternoon, in the summer of 1972, Jackie and I went uptown on the subway. We had an appointment with a notorious doctor whose entire practice was giving people vitamin B_{12} shots laced with speed. He was also going to write a prescription for amphetamines for Jackie. Absolutely everybody was going to this doctor for drugs. We would make an appointment for early afternoon, go in, he would shoot us up with speed, and we would be so high we would walk the sixty blocks back downtown. It was always a real adventure. So we went uptown and got off the subway at Sixty-eighth Street, and as soon as we came upstairs we noticed this woman walking in front of us. She was wearing these very practical men's slacks with a perfect crease down the center, a black turtleneck, and very large sunglasses. She had a knit cap over her head with her hair peeking out. Jackie said, "Oh my God!," and hurried his step up a little to get a peek at her from the side, then he fell back and grabbed my arm and said, "Mona, it's *her*! It's Greta Garbo!" Jackie had met Garbo four years before at a party given by Andy Warhol, and he just adored her. I couldn't believe my eyes, that the divine Garbo was there walking in front of me.

We followed her, but stayed back at a respectful distance so she wouldn't think we were stalkers. Over on Lexington Avenue, she stopped at a florist shop to admire the flowers displayed outside on the sidewalk. I was really shy and stayed back, kind of hiding behind a lamppost, but Jackie went right up to her. And Garbo turned around, startled, and said, "Why, Jackie Curtis! What have you been doing with yourself lately?" And Jackie said, "Oh, not much, I'd like you to meet my best friend, Mona," and made me come up to meet her, and I was just speechless. Garbo was so beautiful, and here she was talking to us! Jackie said, "We'd like to buy you some flowers, which ones are your favorite?" And Garbo said, "Oh, that is so sweet of you, but I'm just really window-shopping today." And we were kind of grateful, because we would have gladly spent all of our speed money on flowers for Garbo.

Holly Woodlawn

In 1965, Jackie had been an usher at Broadway's Winter Garden where Barbra Streisand was appearing in *Funny Girl*, and he was just obsessed with Barbra. So Curtis bought this wig, and it was cut and styled just like Barbra Streisand's hair, and he wore it all the time to Max's Kansas City. Instead of taking it to a hairdresser like normal people do, Jackie would style it himself. One day, before we were going out, I watched him comb the wig himself, and then to set it he sprayed it with this awful-smelling stuff. I looked and it was a can of Raid pesticide—roach spray! I said, "Jackie, what are you doing?," and he said, "Well, there are cockroaches in this apartment. This way, I can kill two birds with one stone." Apparently, Jackie had had the supreme embarrassment one night at Max's Kansas City of having a cockroach crawl out of his wig and down his back. But, really, that wig smelled horrible, just like roach spray.

We would go to the Laundromat with a handful of quarters. Not Jackie. Jackie would just get into the bathtub wearing her dress and stockings and wiggle around, soaking herself in the suds! I would walk in and see this and say, "Jackie, what are you doing?," and she'd say, "I'm not going to spend money on doing laundry." When she felt that her gown was clean enough, she would just unplug the drain and then stand up and blot herself dry with towels and walk around the apartment dripping water everywhere in this dead dress, which now looked even more horrible!

Ellen Stewart

Jackie was very beautiful. He was like a chameleon. When he transformed himself, he was one of the most beautiful women, charming women, sexy women that you would ever have seen. And, in fact, Jackie and Candy Darling, when they both were here—modeled clothing and jewelry for *Vogue* and *Harper's Bazaar*.

Sylvia Miles

Before I met Jackie, I shot some scenes for a detective show, I think it was *Naked City*, on location at Slugger Ann's, her grandmother's tavern. And during that shoot I met Slugger, and I remember she asked me if I had met her grandson Jackie, who was an actress.

I shot *Midnight Cowboy* in 1968. There was a scene where Joe Buck and Ratso are invited to a Warhol party. Viva and Paul Morrissey were in that scene, and I met them. John Schlesinger was very friendly with Andy and [Francesco] Scavullo, and there were a lot of parties during the making of the film. Jackie Curtis and Candy Darling came to every party, and I got to know them. That was really my introduction to the Warhol crowd.

Jackie Curtis had her own style. It was the difference between, what you might say, a sketch and a completed painting. For example, I am wearing pins and rings and a necklace and a watch and bracelets and a hat with a lot of things I've collected over the years, and the ensemble is complete. From whatever angle you catch me, I'm a completely dressed female. Jackie would just do little touches, a wig, a little glitter, some lipstick, and a dress.

Jackie was like the tough girl with the painted lips and rouge. Like a character out of a pulp fiction novel, a tough one that would say, "Blow off, you geezer!" Jackie always used her own voice. Jackie's voice was the same whether he was dressed as a man or as a woman. It's the same voice and the same physicality, the same stride, whether he's a man or a woman. And that was all part of Jackie's unique style.

Holly Woodlawn

I remember one Friday afternoon, Jackie and I had been doing a lot of speed, and we decided to get dressed and do our makeup and go to Max's Kansas City. Jackie used one mirror, I went to another. I started making up one eye, and, three hours later, I was still working on it. My arm became so tired I couldn't hold it up anymore, so we sat down on the couch and worked on each other's faces. By the time we finally got our faces made up to our satisfaction, we looked at the clock and realized Max's was closed because it was 4:30 A.M. So we just stayed home and listened to Barbra Streisand albums, and the rest is history.

Leee Black Childers

In all the time I knew her, she never left the door without looking like Jackie Curtis. So you opened the door a crack, thinking it might be a mass murderer, an ax murderer, but instead you have this weird flaming creature, standing there covered with glitter, with her hair all over the place, in clothes that are safety-pinned together. And one of her signature things—which I don't even think she began doing on purpose—all these runs in her stockings.

So one evening there is a knock at my door and it's Jackie. She says, "Can you let me in? I have nowhere to hide; I have to hide out. Everyone thinks I've committed suicide. I threw all my clothes and things in the East River, and they floated downstream. They'll be finding them soon. Everyone has to think I'm dead, and I need a place to hide. Can I hide here?"

I was this kid from Kentucky, and here is this drag queen covered in glitter that has committed fake suicide—I thought, What do I do with this? But, at that time, I didn't know Jackie Curtis well enough to know that everyone would know it was just a Jackie Curtis stunt. Holly Woodlawn showed up at my door a few days later covered in black, with a boa made of black turkey feathers, saying, "I'm in mourning." I said, "Holly, Jackie's right here!" But Holly insisted, "I know, but I must appear to be in mourning," and went like that to Max's Kansas City, in all these black feathers and black chiffon, for a person who everybody knew wasn't dead.

Andrew Amic-Angelo

Jackie loved to accompany friends on everyday errands in drag just for fun, and one afternoon he came shopping with me. We went into this Greek market on Bleecker Street in the West Village for some things. Jackie was in his typical androgynous drag, and this big macho Greek greengrocer came right up to us and said to Jackie, "What are you? A boy or a girl?" And Jackie instantly and angrily responded, "Don't be so obtuse!" Which is a nice way of saying, Don't be so stupid, but of course that word was not in his vocabulary, he had no idea what Jackie had said, and he just laughed and backed down. Jackie was highly intelligent, and it was funny to see how he could so easily use his intellect to overcome small-minded bigots and fools.

Craig Highberger

I grew up in Pittsburgh, Pennsylvania—Andy Warhol's birthplace. My uncle had been in some classes with Warhol at Carnegie Mellon University, so in the late 1960s I was very aware of Warhol's work and the scene in New York. When I was a senior in high school, I went to campus showings of Warhol's films, and that's where I first became fascinated with Jackie Curtis, Candy Darling, and Holly Woodlawn. I had been making Super-8 movies throughout high school, and, luckily, a film I made about drug use and the generation gap won an award in a PBS competition and helped me get into NYU film school.

Within days of arriving in NYC, in the fall of 1972, I met Jackie Curtis. He was in drag, and came into the basement of my dormitory, the Joseph Weinstein Residence Hall, at 11 University Place near Washington Square, and joined a group of gays and lesbians who were protesting the fact that the university would not allow a gay student group to hold meetings on university property. Jackie was not political, and was probably there because the all-night sit-in was likely to get publicity and news coverage. Wherever there were cameras, Jackie was right there.

I was fascinated with Jackie, and we had immediate rapport. Jackie spent the night in my dorm room because my roommate had not yet arrived. We became good friends, and, for the next thirteen years, I photographed and videotaped his performances. For several years, Jackie frequently crashed at my apartment after a night of carousing. Sometimes, Jackie would stay for a week or so.

Lily Tomlin

Sometimes Jackie and Candy would just kind of drop by Jane's apartment. Or they'd call ahead and say, "We're in the neighborhood!" One thing that was delightful about Jackie was that you never knew how he was going to show up. When he would come to Jane's New York apartment, he might be dressed as a woman or as a man. You never thought twice about it. You sort of envied someone who was able to casually cross that barrier back and forth, and live his life as a kind of performance art.

Sometimes it was a profound turn-on. I would notice everyone getting very sexually disoriented. You weren't sure how you wanted to relate; either you were absolutely in love, or you were going to be totally protective, you wanted to wait on them hand and foot. And if Jackie was in another incarnation, he was like your kid brother.

Holly Woodlawn

Someone had to earn some money, so I applied for and got a position as a salesgirl at the boutique Seventh Heaven, on the seventh floor of Saks Fifth Avenue. They had no clue as to who I was or what I was. So I called Candy and Jackie and said, Get over here, honey—it's winter, wear a big coat, take things into the dressing room, try things on, put the coat on over it, and leave. Don't worry, I'm the salesgirl, I'm not going to call security! So that's what they did, and they went across the street to a cheap bar and I met them there and we had a martini, and they opened their coats and you would not believe how many dresses they had on—at least four apiece! And Jackie immediately would rip every one of them up. And I'm talking about designer dresses, real chiffon, not cheap shit.

Leee Black Childers

We were living on Thirteenth Street and First Avenue, and the bar Slugger Ann's was on Twelfth Street and Second Avenue. So one night we walked a block, and Jackie said, Now, you have to be quiet, and we have to just slip in the door and stand in the shadows, because this is a real bar and we're likely to cause a bit of a stir. So we go in, and there, behind the bar, is this bleached-blond woman with marcelled hair, really styled like the 1930s, and really red lipstick, and thick black mascara, and she's strutting around behind the bar with her hands on her hips. We saw her eyes go to us, and she went over to the old-fashioned register and hit the "No Sale" sign, and it clinged, and the door popped open and she took out a bill and shoved the door shut. Then she squeezed out from behind the bar and came over to the shadows where a drag queen and me stood, and she shoved that twenty-dollar bill in Jackie Curtis's hand. She didn't say a word, but there was kindness and love in her eyes, and she went right back behind the bar and became Slugger Ann again, and we sneaked out of the bar. Today, in 2003, the bar is still there, and looks almost exactly the same as it did more than thirty years ago when it was Slugger's and this happened. Except today it's a gay bar called Dick's. Slugger would just love that.

Paul Ambrose

For many years, Jackie shared an apartment with his grandmother a couple of blocks away from the bar that she ran called Slugger Ann's. One night, Jackie was having sex with this sailor he had picked up and brought back to the place. Jackie was in drag, wearing this Barbra Streisand–styled wig that actually belonged to his grandmother. You can just imagine the scene when Slugger came in after closing the bar up very late on a Saturday night. She walks into her living room and sees Jackie, wearing her wig, in the middle of giving a sailor a blow job. She was probably planning on wearing that wig to church later that morning. Slugger Ann just went ballistic, screaming and smacking Jackie, "Take off the wig, Jack, take off the wig!" Of course, the sailor jumped up and took off into the night.

Holly Woodlawn

One night, Jackie and I left Max's Kansas City around four in the morning, and we were broke so we had to walk back to the apartment we were living in on Tenth Street and First Avenue. This was before it was chic to live there; it was a rough neighborhood back in the early 1970s. So we were walking home, and we both ran out of cigarettes, and all the stores and bars were closed. We had to walk past a fire station across the street. As we approached, we could see someone standing out front smoking a cigarette. And Jackie said, "Holly, wait for me here, I'm going to go get us some cigarettes." And she went across the street and talked to this guy for a minute, and then they both stepped back out of sight into the alley next to the station. I could guess what Miss Curtis was up to.

Well, I stood there by myself for what seemed like forever, and I was getting really nervous because it's 4:30 A.M. and this was not a great neighborhood. I am in this little strapless black dress with sequins, and it's just too dangerous to walk home alone. Suddenly, a car pulls up next to the curb and this creep gets out. He thinks I'm a whore and tries to pick me up. So I run across the street to get away from him and go looking for Jackie. I turn the corner into the alley and there is Jackie in her housedress, with this big burly New York City fireman hugging her from behind. As I get closer, I notice that Miss Curtis's housedress is pulled all the way up in the back, and the front of the fireman's pants are undone. He is plowing her! Right out in the open in this alley! I said, "Oh my God, Jackie, you will do anything for a lousy cigarette. You are disgusting!," and I walked around the corner to the front of the station. A little while later, they walked around the corner, zipping up and brushing themselves off, and I said to the fireman, "Excuse me, do you have a brother?" He said no. "Well, do you have another half hour?" Unfortunately, he didn't. I was incensed that Miss Curtis made out that night and I didn't. At least he gave us what was left of his pack of cigarettes.

Craig Highberger

One night, at 3 A.M., the frantic ringing of my door buzzer awakened me. There was Jackie in drag at my door with a big drunken sailor who had latched onto him, thinking that he was a prostitute. He had Curtis's red lipstick smeared all around his mouth. Jackie looked really scared and immediately asked if I had any cold beer. We planted this big brute on the couch mumbling about his sexual needs, and in the kitchen Jackie said, "Craig, you've got to help me, I can't get rid of him—he wants to fuck me in the ass and I don't want to! He's big and rough and drunk, and I can tell he's going to beat me up or rape me or both. What are we going to do?" I had visions of our bolting, leaving him there, and getting the police, but luckily he passed out cold. I took his arms, Jackie took his legs. We carried him out of the apartment, put him down in the hallway, and locked the door. He was gone the next morning.

Alexis del Lago

You know, one day Jackie telephoned me and said, "I have to take a break—a vacation, I'm coming over to stay with you." At that time, I had a very big apartment on Riverside Drive and Eighty-ninth Street. It was an entire floor of a town house, and it was very fine—high ceilings, chandeliers—and it looked like La Belle Époque. So Jackie arrived with two suitcases of clothes and things. And he had gowns by Yves Saint Laurent, and Oscar de la Renta, all these top designer evening gowns—they were only on loan for a photo shoot Jackie had earlier that month. They were not given to him.

Shortly after arriving and unpacking, Jackie said to me, "Alexis, do you have a scissors?" And I said, Yes, darling, here you are. So in front of my full-length mirror, in my dressing room, he puts on this exquisite, full-length coat by one of these designers and says, "You know, this looks so dumpy," so he takes the scissors and just cuts off both sleeves! Then he put on one of the evening gowns, which was floor-length, and he cut about two feet of fabric off the bottom, making it short, just above the knee. Then he took another dress and cut it to pieces to make a scarf. Watching this, I was wringing my hands; I nearly fainted! He irreparably damaged all these beautiful designer clothes right before my eyes! I shrieked, "Jackie, what are you doing? How are you going to give them back now?" And he shrugged and said, "Oh, don't worry about it—they look better now!" That was Jackie.

Sasha McCaffrey

One night, I found a beautiful Russian sable coat neatly folded over a railing outside a brownstone in the Village. Someone was probably getting in a cab to go to the airport or somewhere and forgot it. It fit me like a glove, and it looked fantastic. It was one of those magic things, like it was meant to be mine. So it was in my closet at home. Now, people were in and out of my place all the time; as many as five people might be living there at any one time. One day, I came home from work, and there, on my front stoop, are Douglas Fisher and Jackie Curtis. Jackie is wearing my Russian sable coat, a red wig, and all the Lucy-red lipstick in the world, smoking a cigarette, and Douglas says, "Shit, there's Sasha, he's going to kill you!" Jackie just said, "Sasha, I wanted to borrow your coat. I was going to ask you, but, it looked so fabulous, I didn't think you'd mind." When Jackie pulled it on, it was obviously too small for her because both of the sleeves had ripped off at the shoulders, and she was showing bare arms from the shoulders to where the sleeves were all bunched up at the forearms.

I said, "Look at that, you've ruined my fur coat, you've ripped the arms off." Jackie said, "What do you mean ruined it? That's the style. Estelle, tell him about style." I said, "Jackie, there's something wrong with you. You're very different. Your mind doesn't work like a normal person's." I knew at that moment that I simply had to decide, Is this the limit? Or am I going to accept and like Jackie for the rest of my life? And the answer was, Yes, I am. It's not logical. You don't know why. It's not because you're bored; it's not because you're just trying to get through whatever circus this is that has been handed to you. Jackie was a very unique person, and completely fascinating.

Joey Preston

One time, Curtis showed up wearing my grandmother's fur coat. And my mother says, Curtis, what are you doing with that coat? He says, "Nana gave this to me, this is my coat," and stamps his foot on the floor, and my dog is barking a mile a minute, [and Curtis is] going, "Beast! Beast! Leave me alone! This is my coat. Nana gave this to me." My mother says, "Curtis, Nana was my mother. When she dies, the clothing goes to me. This is my coat. As soon as you're finished with it, it comes back to me." Curtis pulls the coat tight around him and says, "I don't know what you're talking about, leave me alone, I'm leaving this house."

Another thing that disappeared from the house was a pair of fabulous eyeglasses that my mother had made to order. She really loved unusual eyeglasses. She had shown them to Curtis, but after he left she never saw them again. She figured he'd probably absconded with them. And, sure enough, he wore them as part of his costume in one of his shows. Luckily, I was stage manager. As soon as the show ended, I took them back, and I gave them back to my mother.

Craig Highberger

Andrea Feldman was a rich girl who was one of the stars of Paul Morrissey's *Heat*. She had a trust fund, and her parents set her up in a nice apartment building on Fifth Avenue in the Village. One afternoon, friends arrived to find Andrea sitting in the middle of her living-room floor with a screwdriver, disassembling the window air conditioner. She announced she was looking for hidden microphones. Andrea frequently called herself Andy Warhol's wife, introducing herself alternately as "Andrea Whips Warhol" or "Andrea Whips Feldman." She hung out at Max's Kansas City, where she would frequently leap up onto a table, screaming, "Okay, everybody, it's SHOWTIME!" Then she would screech show tunes off key, while gyrating and stripping, until a bouncer pulled her off the table, kicking and screaming.

There was one infamous night at Max's, in the spring of 1972, when Andrea was in the middle of SHOWTIME. The backroom crowd wasn't really paying attention to her anymore. She had been pulling this stunt for years, and it was getting old. Jackie Curtis walked by the table Andrea was performing on, and Andrea deliberately kicked Jackie in the shoulder. Curtis grabbed Andrea's leg, and she lost her balance and fell to the floor—and got up fighting. Andrea and Jackie tussled, and Jackie's Barbra wig went flying across the room. Andrea grabbed the front of Jackie's housedress and just ripped it completely off. Jackie stood there in Jockey shorts, to which he had safety-pinned his torn stockings! The bouncer dragged Andrea out of Max's, to thunderous applause and laughter, as Jackie tried to safety-pin his dress back together. A few weeks later, just before *Heat* opened, on August 8, 1972, Andrea committed suicide by jumping out of the window of her fourteenth-floor apartment building at Fifth Avenue and Twelfth Street.

Laura de Coppet

I have a memory of Curtis in my kitchen during a party, asking me a lot of questions about Leo Castelli. Castelli was an art dealer who I was seeing at the time. Andy Warhol's art dealer. Leo and I had fallen madly in love in 1976 and started an affair. This was known by quite a few people, and Jackie was very curious and asking a lot of questions, some of which I answered.

I liked Jackie immediately. He was very, very funny. He would come over and would spend the night. He was very high on amphetamines, and we'd talk, talk, talk, talk, until around three or four in the morning. I would be so exhausted, I would say, "Curtis, I have to go to bed." He said, "Oh, that's okay, I have some notebooks here, I'll just stay up and write, sweetheart, you go on to bed." So I did. Now, a boyfriend of mine had given me a case of imported French after-dinner wine, it was like a Sauterne, very, very sweet, and it's meant to be sipped slowly in very small amounts. And it is not cheap. This had been explained to Curtis.

The next morning when I woke up and went into the kitchen, there was Jackie still sitting at the table, and, to my horror, the empty case of wine was just sitting there. In eight hours, while I was sleeping, he drank the entire case of wine. I said, Jackie, do you realize what you have done? And he said, Oh, Ducky, I needed it. I was so high, I needed it to bring me down to write my brilliant new play.

Agosto Machado

One day, Jackie just invited herself to Halston's studio on Fifth Avenue. Halston had the entire floor—way high up, in a building overlooking St. Patrick's Cathedral. And Jackie just walked up to the receptionist and announced, "I'm Jackie Curtis, I'm here to see Halston." And she did it with such flare that they were flabbergasted and went and got Halston. He was just finishing his lunch, and ushered Jackie back to his studio, and Jackie said, "I'm doing my new play, *Americka Cleopatra,* and I would love you to come and see it."

Halston was so caught off guard that he went and cut a huge length of this gorgeous black material, and Jackie stood there, and he draped it around her. It came to Jackie's wrists. Halston pinned it, and cut it here and there, and had one of his seamstresses sew it up, and in less than an hour Jackie was walking out of there with an original Halston gown designed especially for *Americka Cleopatra!* Jackie came to the theater and showed it to everyone, and said, "It needs something." She got a pair of scissors and began cutting it off around the knees. Then she looked in the mirror and said, "Oh, that looks too even." So she just began ripping the fabric. She wore it to Max's Kansas City, and nobody would believe that it was a Halston, or that it had been a Halston. Well, maybe it was a Halston/Jackie Curtis outfit now.

Laura de Coppet

One evening, I went out to a big party with Curtis, and he was cruising. We were separated for a couple of hours, and when I found him later I said, Well, what happened, any luck? And he said, "No, not really—he had a ten-inch dick but a face like a frying pan." I think that's a very funny line.

Alexis del Lago

Jackie had been staying with me for a while in my Riverside Drive apartment, and he said, "Let's throw a big party for all our friends." And I said, But I have so many valuable things, darling, it's like a museum. And he said, We will just take everything breakable and put in the guest bedroom for the party. So we cleared all the bibelots and the objets d'art. And we put candles everywhere, and champagne on ice, and invited Sylvia Miles and Candy Darling and John Vaccaro and Charles Ludlam (who did not come) and all our friends. And I wore a fabulous copy I had made of a Lana Turner gown.

We were there until very very late, and Jackie got very drunk, and even though we had put most of the things away, still, a lot of my things were broken. Nearly all of my 78-rpm records were somehow smashed, and that made me very angry because they were irreplaceable, and I used to play them all the time. That was the first time I had a falling-out with Jackie, and I was very unhappy and didn't talk to him. But he was so cute, before I got up he took everything out of the guest room and put it back in the living room, but he arranged it differently, in his own way. When I woke up, he was gone. He had taken his suitcases and gone. But he left me a thank-you note. He didn't have a telephone, so I took a taxi and I went downtown and found Jackie and I said, "Darling, it looks fabulous, I love what you did to the apartment! You should be an interior designer!"

Michael Musto

I interviewed Jackie at her Fourteenth Street walk-up, which was really kitsch paradise. She told me it was done as a shrine to Maria Montez, the famed B actress, or Z actress, who wanted the cobra jewels. Anyway, *Loving* was on the TV set, but without sound, which is really the best way to watch *Loving*. "Love Me or Leave Me" was playing on the turntable. And she had posters for Lustre Shampoo; she had stacks of unauthorized Barbra Streisand bios. I wanted to move in immediately. And she really endeared [herself to] me by sitting down and pouring me a cup of molten lava—it was supposed to be coffee but it was from a broken Mr. Coffee, and she added cream and two SugarTwins. It was so delicious, so kitschy, so bad taste, perfect.

Don Herron

In 1976, I was living in California, and I started photographing people in their bathtubs, and I came to New York City and was introduced to Jackie Curtis. Because, at that time, he shared an apartment with a relative, he came to my studio to be photographed in my bathtub. He showed up around lunchtime with a big suitcase and two bottles of vodka. It took him four hours to do the makeup and hair, and during that time he drank all the vodka, and I had to practically put him in the tub. Luckily, we did get a series of good photographs.

Jack Mitchell

I loved photographing Jackie Curtis. Some of my pictures of her epitomize this sort of Clara Bow coming into George Hurrell style of photography that was a big influence on me. Jackie and I had an instant rapport because we were both influenced by the same era of Hollywood films, the thirties and forties.

Jackie called me up and asked me if I would take some pictures. It was pro bono, but I managed to get quite a few of them published in magazines like *After Dark*. Jackie was a good businessperson—she knew what she had to offer, and she went with it. Jackie at that time wore tons of red glitter in her hair, and it went all over the place—it took weeks to get out of the studio carpet, and it was in between the floorboards as well.

The first time that Jackie Curtis came to my studio, on East Seventy-fourth Street in New York, she startled me, not because she arrived in drag but because she had Rolodex cards around her wrist instead of a bracelet. This girl was really organized and knew a lot of people. Jackie was very funny, it was a very calculated gay sense of humor; I remember during one session she referred to K-Y jelly as "Fire Island toothpaste."

Michael Musto

Jackie wasn't only great onstage; Jackie was great as Jackie offstage. He was incredible 24/7. He had that special something. He was a raconteur; he was somebody who, as an interviewer, I cherished—because so many interview subjects just sit there or give one-word answers, or won't reveal anything. If anything, Jackie revealed too much. She told you everything. She told you stuff that she probably didn't even know about until she thought about it to tell an interviewer. And I would just turn on the tape and just let her go, and she would say, "Well, if you could be more specific with the questions." But I was purposely being vague, because you got more out of her just by throwing some generic subject at her and letting her "riff." And, eventually, you would get all the specifics, all the details, you needed. Some of them may not have been true, I'm not so sure. Did she really have a grandmother named Slugger Ann? Did Slugger Ann really dress her like a girl? Did she really meet Nicholas Ray? Was Carol Burnett really her spiritual godmother? Whatever! I believed it! And it made good copy, and that's the important thing.

Rose Royalle

One night, Jackie invited me out, because I guess she couldn't get anybody else on such short notice—Eric Emerson was busy or something. At that time, my persona was my original-born gender, so we looked like a couple. She had an invitation for two to cocktails and a fancy dinner at the Rainbow Room. It was a benefit for the Kidney Association, and Andy Warhol had received an invitation with two tickets and gave them to Curtis because he didn't want to go. We were Lower East Side kids, and we sure didn't want to pass up the chance for free drinks and dinner at the Rainbow Room. So Curtis got all dolled up in all her spangles. She gave me a jacket to wear, because, at that time, I didn't really know how to clean up. I remember sitting next to her at this dinner table of all these fancy-smantzy people, and Curtis suddenly saying, "Eddie, my kidneys are killing me—Eddie, my kidneys are killing me!" And she said this *really* loud in front of all these very proper people during a Kidney Association benefit! It just totally cracked me up; I'll never forget it.

I did go back to her apartment and spent the night there. I was probably so bombed that I just passed out. There was some stubble rubbing. There was very little pocketbook banging. If there was, I don't remember it. I thought it was humorous that I was even there overnight. But then, in the morning, I'll never forget, Curtis [went] to the window and [lit] sparklers, right in the window—to attract all the pretty Latino boys on the street. And that was a riot. Only Curtis could do that.

I think out of the entire crowd she was the most creative, she was doing plays and writing things. You know, Candy was the great beauty, and Holly was the Hollywood type. Jackie didn't care if she had stubble showing, or ripped stockings. That's what I think of when I think of Curtis. My stockings were ripped today, and I thought, "That's very Curtis."

Excerpt from Jackie's Hollywood journal, winter 1976:

It was the very best of films. It was the very worst of films. It must have been four-thirty in the morning when I woke up. I turned on the light over my bed. Did I need air? Did I need water? Did I need a man? Impossible. I went to the bathroom after I drank some pure water and smoked half a cigarette wondering what I had been dreaming about. It's a good thing I fell asleep in my clothes. Now all I had to do was put on my lenses and wrap myself in Marilyn's Mexican beach sweater and hide behind my largest sunglasses and go out into the early morning drizzle and collect my thoughts and my self. I had no makeup on but my face was like a peach and my hair was spun gold. There were very few people out, so I flew up side streets and then headed back home with a feeling I was haunted. Nothing but a single cigarette between now and the afternoon. I shall have to see if I have enough soda in the cupboard, or maybe I can fall asleep again. There is mercy somewhere.

I, the keeper of the television flame, say this to you now. I get up and turn on the tube and I hear some ugly man, seated comfortably, going bald as he speaks, I should really say SQUEAKS...he hardly sounds human, and he has the audacity to say, "There are so many things people can do in this society. People can sit down and write their congressman!" So remember, all of us can sit down and write our congressman...isn't that a comforting thought? Don't think I'm not going to drink more black coffee and smoke more cigarettes.

Reverend Timothy Holder

My parents came to my graduation from college in 1977, at a great old aristocratic university, the University of the South, in Sewanee,

Tennessee. And they announced when they arrived, "We have a surprise for you. It's in the car." And I said, "Oh, how nice of you!," thinking there must be a large package waiting for me. And there certainly was—they had brought my big brother Jackie Curtis down from New York City to Sewanee, Tennessee. And I was really embarrassed, even though he was dressed in a man's suit. I thought, What could my parents have been thinking? I thought, Here goes my life and my career. Here I was headed for a career in politics, or religion, or both, I thought this is going to cost me becoming bishop or governor someday. But it turned out to be a delightful weekend. My friends and colleagues at the university did not quite know what to make of Jackie. But, looking back, he was really just showing that he loved me by being present. And it's one of my favorite memories of a brother I miss so terribly.

Barbara Smiley

I met Jackie Curtis while I was a waitress at the Empire Diner. This was during the winter of 1978 through 1979. I was so enamored with him. He'd come in late, probably the graveyard shift, with his wig askew, looking a bit wiped out, and we'd talk a bit. I'd go see him perform at his grandmother's bar . . . I had a signed copy of one of his flyers up on my wall. He was a very sweet person at a time in the seventies when everyone in New York City seemed a little rough around the edges. I knew nothing of his fame until years later, and I never saw him out of drag. Jackie was a very special person.

Lee Black Childers

One morning, I had been out until 5 A.M. at a club called The Sewer, with a creature called International Crisis, who was a drag queen, and Judy Garland, who wished that she was a drag queen. And I walk in, and there's Jackie, and she's in her old-lady dress, her black stockings with runs all up and down them. She'd been on speed, slapping glitter on everything, teasing her hair, going crazy, and then I walk in the door and I was the willing victim, and she whirls around and screams, "Ha, ha, someday everyone will look like *me!*" And you know what? It came true. You can wear rags pinned together and glitter and smell and still be everyone's idol.

Michael Musto

Jackie was really a great performer; she really had the audience in the palm of her manicured hand. She just walked on stage and radiated that special something that stars have—I don't know what it is, it's indefinable, it's magic, and she had it. And she wasn't interested in squandering it on small, tiny, silly roles. She only wanted to play the large, diva roles. She only wanted to play larger-than-life women. And she never wanted to play a cross-dresser, or a transsexual, or a transvestite; she thought that was boring and stupid. She wanted to play women. And back then, in the eighties, and even before that, it was still a semirevolutionary idea to do that, to have a man in drag playing a woman. It still had levels of subtext and texture and shock value. This was before the *Jerry Springer Show*, before RuPaul had a TV show. It was a whole other era, and it was still innovative.

If Jackie was still around today, and, Lordy, I wish he were—he really could make the drag genre fresh, because he wasn't just a drag queen—it was theater; it was subversive. He brought texture; he brought levels to it. It wasn't just a gimmick. It was a real star up there. And, to this day, he would be able to carry that off and bring freshness to it, despite the fact that—you know, a man in a dress, ho hum. That's not what Jackie was. He was a star in a dress. In fact, he said that he was a superstar in a housedress.

CHAPTER 3

Glamour, Glory, and Gold

Jackie as Nola Noonan and Andrew Amic-Angelo as Johnny Apollo
in the 1974 revival of *Glamour, Glory, and Gold,* on stage at the Fortune Theater,
New York City. (Photo by Craig Highberger)

Jackie

I went to the opening night of the opera, *Antony and Cleopatra*. Leontyne Price was doing Cleopatra. Of course, I couldn't afford a ticket, but I went to Lincoln Center to hang around in the lobby and see the rich people arriving in all their finery. It turned out Lady Bird Johnson was there, and she came out during intermission and was screaming, "How glamorous, all that glitter, and all that gold!," and I thought, Fabulous, there's my title: *Glamour, Glory, and Gold*.

I was writing my play and hanging around at the Cafe La Mama, and I was shy and nobody wanted to know me. Then I met Ron Link, who was a director, and a packer of many bags. And I told him about my play and asked him if he wanted to direct it—and I hadn't even completed it yet. And I actually finished writing *Glamour, Glory, and Gold* on his bed on East Fourth Street. But nobody would do it; Ellen Stewart wouldn't do it at La Mama. So I took it to Bastiano's playwright's workshop. And he played very hard to get, but there wasn't anything very hard to get there, because he had no play on. So that is where we premiered. To great acclaim.

Melba LaRose, Jr.

I went in to audition for *Glamour, Glory, and Gold* in 1967. In the front row sat the director Ron Link and the playwright Jackie, who was a sweet boy just barely out of high school. It was a cold reading. I was cast in one of the smaller parts first. They told me the part of Nola had been written for Helen Hanst, who was a big star of off-off-Broadway at the time. Helen had a job as a switchboard operator at the telephone company, and she would always get off late and come in to rehearsal tired and crabby. So one evening we started without her, Ron had me read her part, and she walked in and Ron was laughing at my performance. She said, "If you think she's so funny why don't you just use her?" And he said, "I think I will!" And she just stormed out, and I had three days to learn the part.

The play was a big hit. The critics came opening night, and we received a rave review in the *New York Times*. Dan Sullivan said I was "Jean Harlow down to the leaden voice and incipient potbelly." Jackie and Candy played my sidekicks. Candy Darling was so beautiful, and nobody knew at the time that Candy was a man, so she was reviewed as a woman: "This is the first impersonation of a female impersonator I have ever seen." We ran for six months to packed houses. The play was covered again in a Dan Sullivan article at the end of the season as one of the highlights of the year.

Jackie had a very boyish look in those days—blond bangs, big shoes, with a shopping bag parked by his chair. This was his look for some time—on the streets and in the play. When he appeared on Joe Franklin's show, he took Joe a Halloween pumpkin in the bag. Jackie was a master of publicity, so he got news about the play into all the big gossip columns, on TV, and anywhere else possible. He besieged them with press releases, phone calls, and visits till they posted something. I remember we would go uptown to all the Broadway shows and stand in the lobby and talk up our show. We would say things to each other like, "It's so fabulous, you have to go downtown, it's the most incredible show and the newest talent!" The idea was that people would overhear us and, hopefully, come and check out our show.

Drugs were not a big thing in 1967. It was the debut production for Jackie, Candy, and myself. We were like young children playing together. Some cast members were taking Dexamyl sometimes because we needed high energy for this show—I was constantly onstage, and the role was demanding both vocally and physically—many times I nearly lost my voice. We did drink some wine backstage, but things had not gotten out of hand. It was later that that came into play. Drugs were the cause of Candy's teeth becoming so bad, but I don't know when exactly she started using—in the seventies. Andy paid for caps, but it was a poor dentist, and they kept falling out. There are many funny stories about that.

In one scene, I was having a fit in a Hollywood dressing room and I was to just randomly throw things. One night, by accident, I picked up a wooden hanger and hurled it and it hit Candy Darling right in the middle of the back as she exited to the dressing room. I could not show a reaction—but I was paralyzed, thinking I had seriously injured Candy. At the end of the show, I ran offstage in horror to see if Candy was all right—but she had been worried about *me* all the time. She claimed she wasn't hurt, but thought, How horrible that Melba has to continue her part when she must be so upset!

Andrew Amic-Angelo

I played three male roles in the 1974 revival of *Glamour, Glory, and Gold* opposite Jackie. Two of these were small roles: Lefty, a one-armed tuba player, and a mobster named Johnny Apollo. I also played Arnie, the film director, which was the male lead in the entire second half of the play.

The first day of rehearsals, Jackie wasn't really in drag. He had on a crewneck sweater, blue jeans, and high heels. He was growing his hair out for the show, but it was in pin curls, with bobby pins all over. He had on a little pancake makeup with five o'clock shadow showing through. Very subtle, for Jackie. We were reading through the script with blocking for the first time, and, as Johnny Apollo, in one scene I had to put my arm around Nola. And I noticed Jackie, or Jackie's sweater, had this odd smell. It wasn't body odor or perfume; it was a scent I couldn't place. And during the next break he said to me, "Oh, by the way, my girlfriend Mona took this sweater and rubbed it all over her pussy." And I said,

"Oh, I was wondering what that odor was!" It sounds insane, but it was Jackie's novel way to get into character. And after rehearsal he took off the sweater and put it in a big plastic bag and twisted it shut to preserve it until next time. It was his Nola Noonan rehearsal sweater, and we all had to get used to it because this female-scented sweater was kind of a talisman that helped him assume the role of this sex goddess.

We rehearsed for months. And, in those days, they broadcast two episodes of *I Love Lucy* every afternoon, and this was Jackie's favorite show, so the rehearsals would be set according to the schedule of the *I Love Lucy* show. And during my key scene as Arnie, we actually wrote a line into the script: "Look at you. You are such a pig! All you do all day long is sit around on your ass watching *I Love Lucy*."

The story line of the play follows Nola Noonan. It's kind of a rags-to-riches-to-Hollywood-has-been story. And I really think Jackie and Candy Darling and Holly Woodlawn lived that almost every day. They started their day all living together in a tenement on the Lower East Side of Manhattan, looking for handouts, scrounging meals from friends, but by evening they were all dolled up and they were off to some opening or to some rich person's party. They were real celebrities, but, like Cinderella, at the end of the night reality returned and they went back to a life of poverty on the Lower East Side.

At one point, we had to stop rehearsing at the Fortune Theater because they rented it out for a month as one of the settings for the movie *The Godfather*, Part II. They really fixed it up nice, with a new paint job, with frescoes on the walls. But we had left our props and costumes, and the stupid production manager just took everything when they finished shooting. Jackie was frantic because his scented sweater was gone, and they took a bunch of hats and props and other things. Our director, Ron Link, was furious, and got on the phone, and, later that day, they let us go to the closed set at the Fillmore East, and we were allowed to go through the wardrobe and property trailers and take whatever belonged to our show. Of course, Jackie and Estelle and Madeline and I didn't bother searching for our old things. We went through the racks and picked out the best things we could find. So our show, with the shoestring budget, had some wonderful period costumes and hats unknowingly provided by Paramount Studios, Hollywood.

Lily Tomlin

Jackie could play a character like Nola Noonan and be histrionic, but in some photographs of Jackie dressed as a woman he has that lingering kind of yearning, that been-there-done-that.... It's the look of someone who has seen the world and is weary of it all, but yet has this sincere sweetness. Those eyes are both innocent and pained, lost and lonely—they reveal the loneliness that an artist like Jackie knows.

Craig Highberger

Jackie's play *Glamour, Glory, and Gold: The Life and Legend of Nola Noonan, Goddess and Star*, which has to be the longest title ever, was written and originally produced in 1967, and also 1968, featuring Candy Darling and Robert De Niro in their first major roles on the stage. The 1974 revival at the Fortune Theater opened the night of Candy Darling's wake—she had died of cancer the night before. The play is very derivative of old movies, but is at times both a satire and a tribute. The lead character, Nola Noonan, tastes fame and is immediately hopelessly addicted, which is really Jackie's story. In the 1974 revival, Jackie played Nola, and Douglas Fisher, billed as Estelle R. Dallas, played her sidekick, Toulouse de la Beaupres. Ron Link, who directed Jackie in *Glamour, Glory, and Gold* and in "Cabaret in the Sky," was from Columbus, Ohio.... Ron, who was also known for directing Divine in *Neon Woman*, left New York for Hollywood in the 1980s where he directed plays. He died tragically in 1999 after routine gallbladder surgery.

I was fortunate to have had the opportunity to videotape the entire play over several nights in May 1974. Jackie's stage presence was phenomenal. With his hair grown out and dyed red, some pancake makeup, false eyelashes, and lipstick, and a 1930s thrift shop dress, Jackie became a completely believable feminine presence. The revival opened to glowing reviews. Critics praised Jackie's performance as perfectly nuanced, and the script as worshipful, understanding, and devastatingly honest about its source material. One reviewer called the show a penetrating analysis of what it's really like to live a dream twenty-four hours a day, never quite reaching the ring on the merry-go-round. That was Jackie's life, and it is very sad that the play hasn't been performed in more than two decades.

I went out with Jackie and Douglas many times for late-night partying after performances of *Glamour, Glory, and Gold*. Jackie was a powerhouse of energy, holding court at Max's Kansas City's back room—maybe he was high on amphetamine or something other than booze, maybe he was over-the-top loud and boisterous sometimes, but who cared? Jackie was the best live entertainment in the world, and swept you up in his magic. Both men and women were attracted to Jackie, but, when he was not in drag, many straight men were put off by his feminine qualities. However, when Jackie was in drag, they wouldn't hesitate to interact with him.

GLAMOUR, GLORY, AND GOLD: THE LIFE AND LEGEND OF
NOLA NOONAN, GODDESS AND STAR
A Comedy by
JACKIE CURTIS

Excerpt from Act I—Nola Noonan has just decided to leave her lover Peter Billings, the cop

who put her previous lover, Johnny Apollo, in
jail.

NOLA
(Packing furiously between puffs on a cigarette)
Whaddya want from my life? I tried it your way.
I made an attempt, and everything. I stuck my neck
out on a lotta limbs for you. I reached out and
everything. I fed you hot coffee on the bad nights,
and cold beer on the good nights. You know how I
tried.

I been busting my chops left and right, smiling
at all your cop friends. The same flat feet that
stuck Johnny Apollo away to rot for twenty years.
Well, I've run outta smiles.
(He gets close to her. A touch)
No, Peter, don't.

PETER
Why?

NOLA
You're on duty . . .

PETER
Look, Nola, you never stopped to think why
they stuck Apollo away, and you certainly didn't
care when it happened.

NOLA
(Fingering her necklace)
Boy, you got a bad habit of bringing up the
past. Well, I can't live in the past. Peter, I tried to

be sophisticated. All these months, didn't I peddle tickets for the policeman's ball? That drag!

And didn't I perform at the damn thing? You think special material comes cheap? And how about me serving punch to all those cops and their wives! And your perverted commissioner grabbing my ass backstage. Just so you could get a raise. Peter, I never said anything . . . I Just grinned and beared it.

But you don't care if I never become a movie star. You wanna see me rot away here. You'd like to see me fall away here in this railroad flat with you and Toulouse and that secondhand hot plate!

PETER

All right, Nola, all right.

NOLA

No, it's not all right, Nola, it's not all right! I haven't been to the beauty parlor in months! And when I do one tiny little innocent thing like hire a speech teacher to help me with my "t's," you blow up!

PETER

What's wrong with your "t's"?

NOLA

They're not movie star "t's." You know that. Don't get vague with me!

PETER

What's with you and this movie star mystique, anyway?

NOLA

(With mounting hysteria)

Peter, I never lied to you. We both got into this thing with our two eyes open. I never led you on, and it's been that way ever since that heavenly night in the paddy wagon. I always had a weakness for paddy wagons, you know that . . .

(She drops her cigarette and stamps it out)

Ahh, never mind! When I met you, I forgot about the others. I thought you were my chance, My ticket outta the misery I was in. But now, when you show me two tickets to St. Paul . . . I can't go with you to St. Paul to meet your sister and brother-in-law.

I just don't think I'm the type of girl you could bring home to your sister . . . your brother-in-law, maybe . . . but not your sister. What would they think of a . . . a . . . a . . .

PETER

A stripper?

NOLA

An artiste!

(Nola cries)

Ahh, I'm just a little nobody. What do I have to offer? A facade, a glittering facade?

(She regains her composure)

I can't go to St. Paul with you, or anywhere else. I gotta go to Hollywood. While there still is a Hollywood.

BLACKOUT.

Craig Highberger

Jackie received excellent reviews for *Glamour, Glory, and Gold* when it opened in 1967 at Bastiano's Theater on Waverly Place. The *New York Times* reviewer wrote: "It is written and played with the outrageous broadness of a Gay Nineties melodrama, and in its heartless, campy ramshackle way it is fun." The *Daily News* reviewer called it "... an amusing spoof of Jean Harlow, the studio chief he-man who is actually effeminate, and all the absurd demi-gods the system created," and recommended the play as "an excursion in high camp." The 1974 revival, at the Fortune Theater, was also applauded. The *New York Times* reviewer wrote: "Jackie Curtis can write. The star can also act, bruising friend and foe alike with tense credibility," calling the play "... a savage, wise farce." The *Soho Weekly News* called Jackie's performance "... the performance of the year, in one of the scripts of the year, and Ron Link's carefully honed direction makes it one of the productions of the year." The *Village Voice* had high praise for Jackie's performance as Nola Noonan: "His talent is ineffable and contradictory—he is somehow truthful and touching even when the material is trashy and patently false; he is graceful in his clumsiness, beautiful in his plainness, in control of his knockabout freedom; he plays a woman without pretending to be a woman."

Robert Heide

The real question is, Does anybody know Jackie Curtis? Is Jackie sometimes Barbara Stanwyck? Is Jackie sometimes James Dean? There's a mystery there. My first meeting with Jackie was through Ron Link, who was directing Jackie's play *Glamour, Glory, and Gold*. Candy Darling was one of the stars, and her hair was still the original brown and her teeth were not yet fixed. Jackie was just a quiet, shy boy, and, at that time, he had flawless skin. Ron Link was doing his usual slam-bam directing and cursing everybody out. I remember him arguing with Jackie a lot. There was a lot of fighting going on. But that was part of the play, and some of it spilled over. Ron was kind of a Warner Baxter control freak kind of director.

Jackie hadn't yet developed the persona that we all came to expect, whether it was Barbara Stanwyck or James Dean. That melodramatic persona allowed Jackie to emerge in the same sense that people emerged through the Angels of Light—it was a time of gender-bender. We're talking about the sixties, when all hell was breaking loose.

Craig Highberger

One night after a performance of *Glamour, Glory, and Gold*, Jackie and Estelle decided to wear their costumes and full makeup home. They had the cash from the night's performance (the show was considered a "showcase" and so admission was free, but the actors stood at the door after the show and collected donations in a hat, which were divided among cast and crew). They decided to save cab fare and walk, stopping in every Lower East Side dive for a drink along the way.

At some point, three Puerto Rican youths started hassling the girls, and one had a switchblade that he held against Jackie's bare back. The knife nicked Jackie. The wound, which was small and seemed to heal quickly, actually caused an internal infection. Jackie hated doctors and did not go to one, even when blood appeared in his urine a week later. Several nights later, he collapsed on stage during a performance and was taken to the emergency room. After running some tests, a surgeon performed emergency surgery to remove one of Jackie's kidneys, which had been destroyed by infection.

Andrew Amic-Angelo

The most challenging part of my role as Arnie the director in *Glamour, Glory, and Gold* was an incredible ten-minute monologue, really a long tirade, where I criticize my screen goddess Nola Noonan endlessly. I threaten her and lash out at her over and over again, enumerating all her failings, and she just sits there and absorbs every insult until I finally wind down, and then she rises up indignantly. It is a brilliant scene. The power shifts completely to her, and it really is a brilliant piece of writing.

> Excerpt from Act II—Arnie's angry monologue
> after drunk Nola Noonan behaves outrageously
> on the set during filming of *Goddess of the Reich*.

ARNIE
(Bending Nola's arm behind her back)
Nola, sweetie, honey, baby, darling, poopie . . . get this! And get it straight. Your language is costing the studio valuable prestige. This is not the old days, and it's not like old times when Nola could come in and bitch to just anyone living . . . no. These are hard times. People are forming breadlines.

NOLA
(Breaking free of Arnie's grasp)
Let 'em eat cake!

ARNIE
Look at you! Take a good look at you!!
(Nola quietly sits and listens to Arnie)
You're beginning to smell like a rummie . . . a

lush. You already look like an aging character actress on her way to the glue factory. You've forgotten what it means to have to have continents at your pretty, pedicured, perfumed little feet.... Look at those feet. Look at those fucking feet! If they're not swollen, they're black-and-blued, or you got them in Ace bandages so tight ... I ought to slap the shit out of you and bind those fucking feet!

You're amazing ... I've never seen such a pig! And what do you do, Porky? You sit around on your ass all day watching *I Love Lucy*. Ah, yes. Stars are stars, and stars will have outrageous private lives ... so outrageous that even I can't keep them out of the newspapers! I warned you once. I warned you twice. I warned you three ... four times after that, I remember. And yet, what does the property man find in your purse? Gin, gin, gin! Gin-soaked, rotting, smelly, sweaty Nola Noonan ... how does that sound? A diseased camel smells better than you do! But you go right on, pouring that cheap, French perfume all over your clothes. It's getting so bad I can hardly distinguish the perfume from your unbelievably offensive B.O. And I don't mean Box Office, bitch! And when was the last time you shaved your legs? Brushed your teeth? Gargled ... chewed a piece of sweet, smelly, tasty chewing gum ... and when was the last time you went to confession, Nola?

But they say with age, there comes the closest relative: senility. Get it, sweetie? Senility's setting in with you. Face it, Nola, you've had it! Even Toulouse says you're through. You've changed, Nola. You've lost a great deal of that innocence you displayed so early in your career . . . but soon replaced by a cute drinking habit.

Boy, what plans I had for you. . . . You were gonna be big time, big top, honey! You and that schmuck sidekick of yours. I'm speechless, Nola, absolutely speechless! You turned out to be a real hard case, how do you say . . . a real mean mother-fucker! Wow, am I hurting. Well, get this and get it straight, just in case you forgot . . . your silver lin-ing is tarnished . . . shot.

Go on and shake, you rat bastard, drink, drink, drink, smoke, let them feel your legs up. What the fuck do you care? You're stoned and out of your head most of the time. You can't remember whether you're walking on air, a tightrope, or thin ice. But I'm warning you, Nola, and I'll be brief . . . watch out . . . just watch out . . . you can only push me too far before I bust. I'm a regular kind of a guy. If you're a regular kind of a girl . . . then we under-stand one another? Then, we do business.

Your fans don't want to pay five bucks to see a pair of sagging tits on a smelly slob in pink se-quins. Bad enough we have to put up with those friends of yours. The loudest queens in Hollywood. Do you know what I heard the grips call your costars? "A couple of talented cocksuckers." How do you like that? But I put up with them . . . Why? Because your name alone on any flyer, kiosk, or marquee anywhere in the world today evokes such a devastating and intoxicating spell for millions of men everywhere.

Oh, there's no getting around it without run-ning into the girl on cloud nine . . . why don't you face it, Nola? You've only got a few good pictures left in you, maybe, with a nice long rest without any of de boozie-booze. Maybe then you could get back on that set without falling flat on your god-damned face. Today, you fell on your face ... or was it your ass? Come to think of it, Nola, it's getting mighty hard to tell which is your face and which is your ass.

(The cast laughs at this)

Quiet! At first, it was funny. The audiences thought it was a novelty act. You know, part of the show? Well, you no longer amuse anybody ... you're fucking repulsive! Do you even know what it means to be fucking repulsive? You are gonna suffer, Nola.

It don't take no crystal ball to figure out where you'll wind up ... the bins! The loony bins! In between flops, that's where they'll have to keep you ... just so they can keep you from killing yourself. And every day a little bit of your mind disappears.

(He makes an air sound)

Whoosh! And I really think your brain cells have been anaesthetized from your sleazy environment. Go ahead and drink ... and then tell me something, Nola: After you piss away every female hormone in your decaying body, then what? What the fuck then, huh?

Oh, I don't know about you anymore, Nola. I just can't put up with you anymore. My patience with you is at a low ebb. You what that means, ya dumb cunt?! Anytime you feel like you wanna take a nice long walk somewhere else, you go right ahead ... But if you insist on drinking yourself to death, kindly do it on your own time! I pay people to make pictures... I don't pay people to drink and sweat in my company.

(He lifts her arm)

Awwwww! Look at that! What a fucking mess you are! You smell, you sonofabitch! You stink...

NOLA

I hate you!

(Finally moving from her chair)

I hate you! And I will never talk to you again, as long as I live, which will be forever. You put me up on that silver screen, and then you dragged me down again.

(She goes right up and leans over Arnie's shoulder)

Arnie, tell me... how does it feel to play GOD?

ARNIE

(Shoving Nola away)

It hurts, Nola. It hurts.

NOLA

That's great. Hit a woman when she's drunk.

TOULOUSE

You don't understand, Arnie. Comebacks are a very delicate operation.

NOLA

(Going for Toulouse)

Comeback... COMEBACK... There's that WORD again!

(She throws Toulouse down)
Get this and get it straight—there is NOTH-
ING delicate about Nola Noonan!
(She kicks Toulouse)
And that's for not calling the liquor store!

BLACKOUT.

Andrew Amic-Angelo

Nola Noonan's sidekick in *Glamour, Glory, and Gold* was Toulouse de la Beaupres, played by one of Jackie's oldest friends, Douglas Fisher. Douglas billed himself as Estelle R. Dallas in play programs or whenever he went around in drag. Douglas was a notorious alcoholic, and one night during the run of the play Jackie and I were doing a scene and Toulouse's entrance was coming up. And Mona Robson was backstage dressing Estelle, and I heard this commotion. I look offstage into the wings and see Douglas rip his dress off. He throws it at Mona's feet and storms out. He just walked out of the theater, right in the middle of the show! And there wasn't an understudy. We had half of the play to finish, and the character of Toulouse is all through it. So Jackie looks at me, and I look at Jackie, and we just continued, and we just worked Toulouse's lines into our own. It was amazing that we were able to do that, paraphrasing the missing character's content. It was kind of exciting to kind of rewrite the rest of the show extemporaneously.

Craig Highberger

The night Douglas Fisher walked out on the show in the middle of the performance, he had been very drunk on stage. So drunk that he missed cues and forgot lines. After the show, I went to Phebe's with Jackie and a few of the other cast members, and Douglas was already there drinking. When we came in, he saw us, but he sheepishly turned away. We ignored him completely. A few minutes later, a nice young woman we all knew went up to Douglas at the bar. Before we knew it, for no reason, he ripped her glasses off of her face, broke the frames in half, threw them on the floor at her feet, and stomped on them, while going off in an insane tirade at her. The bouncer rushed over and picked Douglas up and threw him out the door onto the sidewalk. Ron Link wanted to fire Douglas, but he was contrite, and Jackie was a loyal and almost too forgiving friend. Douglas finished the run, but it was the last time he would be cast in any kind of a substantial role in a Curtis play.

Andrew Amic-Angelo

During the 1974 run of *Glamour, Glory, and Gold*, I accompanied Jackie and Ron Link to a taping of a cable-access show. It was shot in a basement nightclub on Macdougal Street late at night. Jackie was in drag—in fact, he came straight from the performance, after a pit stop at the bar. The female host of the program was hostile and questioned Jackie very harshly, asking why he would want to dress as a woman. She asked him, "Why don't you just have a sex change operation and become a woman?" Jackie was put off by her attitude, and replied, "Why would I want to be anything less than what I already am?" The host was speechless and ended the interview.

CHAPTER 4

Americka Cleopatra, Heaven Grand in Amber Orbit, and Everything in Between

Agosto Machado and Jackie Curtis in *Americka Cleopatra* (1972).
(Agosto Machado Collection)

John Vaccaro

I came to New York at the beginning of the whole pop art movement. I began my theater company in the mid-sixties; 1965, in fact. We called it the Play-House of the Ridiculous. Nobody was thinking about making money. We were putting on shows. We were artists. What we were doing was an entirely different type of theater. It was truly experimental. There's nothing experimental now. I recently went to see *Urinetown*. What a piece of shit; it's about nothing at all.

Theater is just not the same today. They're not interested in what we were doing. Today, you can't even afford to do off-off-Broadway. Nowadays, they want five thousand to ten thousand dollars a week just for the venue. We did entire shows for twenty dollars! My first shows, I didn't even have theater lights. You just turned them on and off like a regular household switch. I didn't have anybody designing costumes. We did the costumes. We used to go to the area they now call SoHo where there were all these fabric places that would throw stuff out. We would take the fabric remnants and use them to make costumes. And as for sets—we did it like Louise Nevelson did, with found objects.

Jackie was in one of my plays called *The Life of Lady Godiva*. And we were invited to perform at the first pornographic festival at the University of Notre Dame. And being a romanticist, I decided that we would go by train. Jackie was late, and showed up, for the first time, in drag in public. And we went on the train to South Bend, Indiana. We had arrived and we were hungry and we went to this restaurant—and everyone knew that Jackie was in drag. Jackie got up to go to the bathroom, and everybody stopped and watched. And Jackie, of course, went right into the ladies' room.

Ruby Lynn Reyner

I appeared in John Vaccaro's Play-House of the Ridiculous production of *The Life of Lady Godiva*, by Ronald Tavel, with Jackie. Notre Dame, a Catholic university in Indiana, invited us to perform the show for a big conference called "Pornography and Censorship," and the entire cast went there on the train. We were so excited. Jackie and I were like Rita Hayworth in 1940s dresses, sitting on our luggage in Grand Central station with our legs crossed, waiting to be photographed. It was on that train trip that Jackie began writing *Heaven Grand in Amber Orbit*. He found a racing form on his seat in the diner car, and he came up with most of the characters' names from it, like Classie Gravesend and Rouge Frolic—those were the names of racehorses!

So we got to Notre Dame. It turned out our performance caused such a stir that they censored us! *Lady Godiva* was quite risqué, even for the late sixties, with lots of nudity and crazy scenes with nuns fucking each other. The university made us keep our clothes on, so we simulated all these sex acts in costume. After the show, there was a big party for us at the student union, and all these Notre Dame college boys were so fascinated with Jackie I remember it made me jealous.

Alexis del Lago

I met Jackie Curtis in 1968. He was doing a show, and a friend of mine brought me backstage. And when I arrived, I was in an exquisite gold lamé outfit—any other diva would have hated me! Not Jackie. Jackie admired me, appreciated me—we became great friends, and I was asked to be in the show *Americka Cleopatra*. I played Charmin Gale.

I saved one of the reviews in my scrapbook. It begins: "The Theatre of the Lost Continent's latest production stars Jackie

Curtis and was, I'm sorry to say, uneven, frenetic, and a bit of a hodge-podge affair. Despite the mishmash production there were some excellent performances turned in. Alexis del Lago was delicious as Charmin Gale and Agosto Machado was absolutely hilarious as the rubber-titted lady-in-waiting. Good ole Harvey Fierstein was brilliant as Cleo's Jewish mother. Jackie Curtis is, after all, Jackie Curtis. His/her performance was a gum-chewing, crack-snapping one, which only he/she could have brought off."

This is their opinion, darling. They're reviewing this as if it were a Broadway show—*Americka Cleopatra* was avant-garde. Everybody was there—the theater was packed, you couldn't have walked in, it was sold out! Jackie was brilliant. Jackie had so many facets, like a diamond. It was wonderful to see him perform.

By the end of the run, Jackie and I had become great friends. At that time, he lived on Second Avenue and Twelfth Street, in a big loft on top of a movie house. Every Friday and Saturday, we would put on shows. Jackie always admired my dresses because we had the same taste—we both loved Garbo and Dietrich and the only one: Maria Montez. So I made him a beautiful wraparound dress in aubergine velvet and gold and brought it to him as a present. He loved it. So that Friday night when we did the show, I thought he would wear it, but at the finale there was Wilhelmina Ross wearing it! I went up to her and said, "What are you doing with that? That's my dress—that's Jackie's dress!" But Jackie was Jackie, and we loved him.

Styles Caldwell

Jackie wrote this fabulous comedy *Americka Cleopatra*. I remember Harvey Tavel directed it. In my opinion, Jackie always got the wrong people to put on his shows, and then there would be problems because they would try to change it and do it their way instead of Jackie's way. Jackie should have been directing and controlling the shows himself, but he couldn't do everything. So there were always conflicts and arguments between Jackie and whoever was directing.

I was in the show and played Valerie Nash; that was the name of a racehorse Jackie found in the *Racing Form*. I was Mrs. Julius Caesar. Agosto Machado and Alexis del Lago were Cleopatra's handmaidens. Harvey Fierstein played Cleopatra's Jewish mother. This is avant-garde off-off-Broadway theater, but Tavel insisted upon trying to stage it like a straight uptown Broadway show. He wanted to make Jackie gorgeous, which just isn't Jackie's style at all. I remember at dress rehearsal Jackie came out in a fabulous outfit that he got from Halston and modified and accessorized. He had a curtain rod on his head with a beaded curtain hanging down to the floor, and it was just fabulous, but Tavel was appalled, and whined, "Oh, this is just awful. I wanted to make him so beautiful." Tavel had some dance director who had been in *Sextette* with Mae West, and he tried to get us to learn all these intricate dance steps. None of us were interested in becoming professional dancers, so that didn't work. The show was fabulous anyway. . . . Without telling his grandmother, Jackie had borrowed a bunch of her old outfits—dresses from the thirties—and several of us had on her things. On opening night, Slugger Ann was in the audience, and as soon as the curtain went up she loudly exclaimed, "They're wearing my fucking clothes!" It was a huge success, and we were sold out every night for the entire run.

Agosto Machado

One Saturday afternoon, we all came to the theater for our rehearsal for *Americka Cleopatra*, and Jackie had just watched the Roy Rogers children's western show on Saturday-morning TV, and she had decided that Dale Evans in all her cowgirl regalia was sort of an American version of the Egyptian Cleopatra, or that Cleopatra was sort of the Dale Evans of her time.

Jackie had braided her hair, she wore Levi's and a little bolero, and she had two cap pistols in a holster slung low around her waist. It did not faze me in the least. It was brilliant. There are people that aren't used to downtown theater who were taken aback and didn't know how to react. Jackie could create magic and a mood. People dismiss it as not being disciplined, but in the fine art of theater and performance it was unique. If you want to see the same old mundane formulaic thing, go to Broadway, God bless 'em. The reviews are like what you see. Sixteen years later, twenty-three years later, that's the show. Jackie's plays were different; they were alive, and changed during the run, and always had immediacy and the element of the unexpected.

Harvey Fierstein

Americka Cleopatra was a very long script with a lot of scenes, some of which had something to do with Cleopatra. A lot of it didn't. We cast all of our friends—Alexis del Lago and Agosto Machado. I played Jackie's mother; "Incredibe" was my name. My big scene was when Cleopatra had gone off to Las Vegas with Caesar. He had eloped with my much younger daughter, and I show up the morning after the wedding night to blackmail him. It was a brilliantly funny scene, and Jackie was supposed to be asleep in the wedding bed while Caesar and I had it out.

The more laughs I got playing this scene, the less willing Jackie was to stay asleep during it. She would start sitting up, making faces, during it, and I would hit her with my purse to get her to lie down again. So after a few performances like this, I went to Jackie and I said, Look, am I doing this scene wrong? Because I think this is one of the best things you've ever written. This is a solid scene that Neil Simon would be thrilled with, had he written it. The jokes are brilliant; it's one after another—zinger, zinger, zinger. You're not stealing lines from other people, it's not pastiche, it's original, it's funny, it's Woody Allen–worthy material. But I must be doing it badly, because you keep interrupting the scene. And he said, No, you really do it wonderfully. And Jackie never moved again during that scene.

Jackie was always stealing everybody's makeup. And he cut up the Halston dress with a pair of scissors before our eyes and just made a total mess of it. And then one night during the run of *Americka Cleopatra*, while I was out on stage, he sat down at my dressing table to use my makeup. And he took his wig off and put it down, but he didn't realize that the 100-watt lightbulbs around my mirror were really hot. And this gorgeous wig just melted onto the lightbulbs. Damn if he didn't wear it on stage like that! It was a horrible mess, and it smelled like burning rubber. But that was Jackie.

Paul Serrato

Jackie had learned that I was a composer and a musician, and asked me to write the music for a show he had written based on the life of Tommy Manville. Manville was heir to an industrial fortune, and Jackie was smitten with one aspect of his life: the fact that Tommy Manville, for all his money, was a big playboy, and he loved chorus girls and marrying chorus girls. So this seemed ready-made for a musical. Jackie, of course, would be playing the part of Tommy Manville. The show was called *Lucky Wonderful* because Jackie couldn't use Tommy Manville's real name. The show was a hit, and Jackie's reputation as a writer and a comic performer was very quickly growing at that time.

Melba LaRose, Jr.

I was in Jackie's second play, *Lucky Wonderful*, in 1968. It was a musical take on Tommy Manville and all his wives, and was done at the Playwrights Workshop, Tony Bastiano's place, a basement on Waverly Place; Tony was often called "La Papa." Jackie played Tommy Manville. Jackie was in his Huntz Hall period, so he was taking male hormones and looked like a curly-haired collegiate trust fund kid in a raccoon coat and big shoes. The show had some great songs by Paul Serrato, including a love ballad, "Who Are You?," that Jackie sang beautifully. Roz Kelly and I played all the women's roles. I played five roles: Ninny Eldorado, a Russian princess with a tarnished crown; Popcorn Collins, a Southern tap-dancing movie star; Norma Lewis, a fallen star; a wacked-out gossip columnist à la Hedda Hopper; and a trashy chorus girl. My big song was "Do You Still Carry a Torch?," and I remember on closing night, for fun, I came out to sing the number carrying a real burning torch. And Jackie, not to be outdone, ran offstage and came back like a waiter with a towel over his arm and a tray with a pitcher of ice water and doused the flame!

Most people could not follow Jackie's train of thought. He was extremely educated and bright, and always exploring new ideas: I remember once he showed me a play he was writing in Esperanto! He wanted me to play a character named Ashes Mercredi. *Mercredi cendres* means "Ash Wednesday" in French, so the name is playing on that. Jackie was one of the most brilliant people I have ever met.

Michael Arian

I knew Jackie from working with John Vaccaro's Play-House of the Ridiculous in the late sixties and early seventies. I worked with him on a play that Jackie wrote called *Heaven Grand in Amber Orbit*, which, like the times in which we lived at that point, was totally inspired by and fueled by drug use. And the legend goes that Jackie had found a wallpaper sample book in the garbage, had taken it home and taken massive amounts of speed, and written a play that pulled lines from movies, from other plays, and put it together as a long string of non sequiturs. When I first saw it as an audience member, I had never seen anything as funny in my entire life. I had to meet the director, and the company—which I did—and I got to work with this company, the Play-House of the Ridiculous.

John Vaccaro

Jackie had an extensive wardrobe, and I'm certain everything was from the thrift shop. I can see him so clearly, in a print house-dress and mesh hose torn beyond belief. But you know I never thought of Jackie as a woman. He was really a very great talent, a great artist.

Jackie Curtis was completely in tune with what we were doing at the Play-House of the Ridiculous. We were really into the movies of the thirties and forties. That's where our sensibility came from. We were especially crazy about the terrible old films of Maria Montez. Jackie wrote a play. People told me he found the script in a litter basket and just put his name to it. And, curiously, the names of the characters in the play were named after horses that he found in a *Racing Form.* "Heaven Grand" was one horse, and "Amber Orbit" was another. Originally, the play was to take place in an old hamburger joint on Forty-second Street. I turned it into a musical. I took it to Europe. For two or three years, we toured with it.

I remember after one of the rehearsals we were walking up to Max's Kansas City. Jackie had on torn hose and a thirties dress from a thrift shop, and somebody came up and said, "Hey, are you a real woman?" And Jackie said, "Do you think a real woman would dress like this?" Jackie had a great sense of humor about himself.

Craig Highberger

Written over the course of two years, 1967 to 1968, *Heaven Grand in Amber Orbit* is an experimental work of genius. It is to the stage play form what William Burroughs's "cut-up" work—when he would cut up printed materials and rearrange the lines and segments to create a new work—was to the novel.

For *Heaven Grand in Amber Orbit*, Jackie Curtis, fueled by copious amounts of amphetamine, took lines and dialogue fragments from old movies, television commercials, songs, novels, and other plays and pulled it all together into a manic stage play that stunned audiences. Even the play title is derivative, taken from an edition of the *Racing Form*. "Heaven Grand" was the name of one racehorse; "Amber Orbit" was another.

John Vaccaro, founder and director of the Play-House of the Ridiculous, first produced and directed the work in November 1969. It was an immediate smash hit. Vaccaro was recognized as one of the mad geniuses of the American theater. Jackie started the run of the play in the lead role of Heaven Grand. Holly Woodlawn played a Moon Reindeer Girl, and remembers they had to slather her entire body with Vaseline petroleum jelly, which was then covered in silver glitter. Many members of the cast were using speed and other intoxicating agents during the performance. Many people remember the infamous night when Holly was so high she simply could not articulate her lines—so whenever one of her lines came up another player would nudge her, and Holly, instead of delivering the line, simply went "WA—WA—WA—WA—WA—WA—WA—WA—WA!" in kind of an insane riff on the concluding scene from *The Miracle Worker*. Both the audience and players went into hysterics because Holly was so obviously, and hilariously, inebriated.

From the very beginning, Jackie Curtis and John Vaccaro had

serious disagreements about the play that quickly escalated into arguments. One day, in a fit of anger, Vaccaro ripped Jackie's costume to shreds, and fired him from the production. Ruby Lynn Reyner was Curtis's replacement.

Vaccaro turned the play into a musical. He added hilarious touches: Jackie's royal matriarch character, named Lady Galaxy, was originally to occupy an onstage throne throughout the play; Vaccaro replaced it with an old discarded toilet found in the trash. Jackie's genius as a playwright and Vaccaro's aplomb as a director combined to make a unique work that played several months in New York, to packed houses.

HEAVEN GRAND IN AMBER ORBIT: THE CAB FARE GIRL
A comedy by
JACKIE CURTIS

Cast of Characters
Heaven Grand in Amber Orbit, the heroine
Nightcloud, the hero
The Rouge Frolic, a mad menace
Lady Galaxy, ruler of Casio Octavio
Lord Pass-the-Hat (pass-the-hat)
Princess Ninga Flinga Dung, the Queen of Song
Glamour Man, behind those Foster Grants
Rhumba Line Sam, the barker
Midnight Marie, a lady of the evening
Millie Mae, ditto
Madcap Betty, ditto
Classie Gravesend, a henchman
Dapper Dare, a john
Crystal Palace, a madame
Shinola, a maid

Sacra Via, the sex change, a token
Terra Rubra, the nice nurse
Tourists, old women
And introducing Eve Harrington as
Margo Channing.

Excerpt from Act I—Millie Mae, Madcap Betty, and Midnite Marie, three ladies of the evening, enter in the guise of musicians, each with their own instrument. They seat themselves, and Lady Galaxy has her musicale.

LADY GALAXY

I don't feel it beneath me to judge the girl, Ladies . . .

MILLIE MAE

But . . .

MADCAP BETTY

Yes?

MIDNITE MARIE

Don't let us stop you, Lady Galaxy. It'll be a long time from now when we ever stop YOU, Lady Galaxy. You are the ruler of Casio Octavio. You wanna judge value, judge value!

LADY GALAXY

(A nod to each girl as she acknowledges
them. Nod)

Millie Mae!

(Nod)

Madcap Betty!
                    (Nod)
Midnite Marie!
                    (Enraged)
Heaven Grand in Amber Orbit will PAY for this!
            (Lord Pass-the-Hat enters)
Lord Pass-the-Hat!

                    LORD
Pass-the-hat!

The Rouge Frolic and Classie Gravesend enter
with Princess Ninga Flinga Dung. They throw her
            down at Lady Galaxy's feet.

                    ROUGE
We discovered her outside your window, my
lady.

                    PRINCESS
                    (Crying)
Sacra Via is coming! Sacra Via is coming!

                    CLASSIE
She is delirious, my lady.

                    ROUGE
The village sun has set her brain on fire!

                    LADY GALAXY
Well, Lord Pass-the-Hat, have you met Princess
Ninga Flinga Dung? The Queen of Song? She is
transformed into a town crier before our very eyes!

PRINCESS
(Stops crying)
If this is your idea of a joke, Lady Galaxy, I . . .

LADY GALAXY
You WHAT?

PRINCESS
I find it extremely difficult to laugh.
(She tries a few laughs, unsuccessfully)

LADY GALAXY
(To Rouge Frolic and Classie Gravesend)
Chain the girl—she is a very swift pain, I find.

LORD
(To Midnite Marie)
Thieving hussy! Gimme my hat, you bitch! I caught you taking my hard-earned pennies! I am Lord Pass-the-Hat, I have majored in Ethiopian Epigrams, sold emery boards in the snow, and am given to hives on Halloween!

MARIE
Oh?

LORD
What have YOU ever done?

NIGHTCLOUD
(To Heaven)
Why do you go on like this?

HEAVEN
(Into phone)
Room service! ROOM service!

Rhumba Line Sam enters and lines up with Millie
Mae, Madcap Betty, and Midnite Marie.

SAM
Ladies, ladies, ladies!

MARIE
No wisecracks, huh?

SAM
Crystal Palace just got word from Silver May-
king, Sacra Via IS coming!

MILLIE MAE
Sacra Via is coming!

MADCAP BETTY
Sacra Via is coming!

MIDNITE MARIE
My ass itches, Rhumba Line Sam. Where's my
foot powder?

PRINCESS
I TOLD you, Sacra Via is coming!

LORD
(To Princess)
Nobody asked you!

SAM

I sent for her!

LADY GALAXY

YOU?! You, who never even sent out for a container of coffee? Tell me—why?

SAM

Why, Lady Galaxy, she is the sun, the moon, and the stars.

LADY GALAXY

She is a sex change, if she exists!

SAM

She is my wife.

PRINCESS
(Overcome)
The IRONY of it all! The IRONY of it all! Sacra Via is coming! Sacra Via is coming! SHE will save Heaven Grand in Amber Orbit!

NIGHTCLOUD

Save me the drumstick.

SAM

Shinola, Shinola!
(Shinola, a maid, enters)

SHINOLA

Yes'm?

SAM

Save Nightcloud the drumstick.

SHINOLA

Oh, yes'm.

(She starts to exit, but pauses and turns back)

But Rhumba Line Sam, even a pimp knows it isn't Thanksgiving. There is no turkey at our table.

SAM

You mean?

      (Shinola nods yes and she exits)

Nightcloud, what grade are you in?

NIGHTCLOUD

Grade A.

SAM

Grade A?

NIGHTCLOUD

Vitamin D. Stretch one!

LADY GALAXY

Milk for Nightcloud!

MILLIE MAE

She looks after that young man too closely.

BETTY

For someone, even Lady Galaxy who claims no kin to the boy, ordering milk is no airy task.

MARIE

(Holding a knife. To Rhumba Line Sam)

The next time you stand me up . . .

(She holds the knife to his privates)

I'll cut your head off!

SAM

I've got a hard-on. Marry me?

MARIE

I beg your pard-on?

SAM

Hard-on. HARD-ON!

MARIE

Lucky for you I majored in English.

SAM

You too, Midnite Marie?

MARIE

Do you . . . still . . . wanna marry me, Rhumba
Line Sam?

SAM

I lost my hard-on.

MARIE

I'm going to jump completely out of character
and say this much—that's what I go for, a straight
yes or no answer!

The Moon Reindeer Girls enter.

MOON REINDEER GIRLS
(Chanting)
Ole-o, le-oleum. Ole-o, le-oleum. Ole-o, le-oleum. Ole-o, le-oleum. Ole-o, le-oleum. Ole-o, le-oleum.

PRINCESS
(Singing)
Nobody knows the trouble I've seen. Nobody knows the trouble I've seen. Nobody knows the trouble I've seen.

HEAVEN
Heartbreak Hotel!

NIGHTCLOUD
Room service! Room service!

LORD
(Hands on Heaven)
If you don't let me fuck you, Heaven Grand in Amber Orbit, you can at least let me use your bathroom.

HEAVEN
Oh, Lord Pass-the-Hat, a person with your Ilka Chase doesn't deserve a second chance.

LORD
Whose side are you on?

NIGHTCLOUD
A side of French!

LORD
French fries, I'll wager.

NIGHTCLOUD
If such a wager be waged. Be it so. Yes, a side of
French fries, if you must know.

HEAVEN
I'm on the Lord's side now, if anyone's still
interested. I checked into this hotel under an as-
sumed name, it's true, but that's half the battle—
admitting it, isn't it? Isn't it?
(Hysterical, she breaks down and cries)

LORD
(To Nightcloud)
How long you been hung like this?

NIGHTCLOUD
Ask me no questions, I'll tell you no lies.

LORD
Oh! An Apache of the law.

DAPPER DARE
(Knocking on door)
Open up! Open up!

CRYSTAL PALACE
I'll make a telephone call first. Be gone!

DAPPER DARE
I must see Heaven Grand in Amber Orbit. Open up!

CRYSTAL PALACE
She's been swallowed by a whale.

DAPPER DARE
That's a whale of a tale.

CRYSTAL PALACE
Or the tail of a whale!
(They laugh)

REINDEER GIRLS
(Singing)
Swing lo, sweet chariot. Coming for to carry me home. Swing lo, sweet chariot. Coming for to carry me home.

PRINCESS
We who are about to die salute you.

There is a fanfare, followed by the entrances of Sacra Via and Glamour Man. Sacra Via is the token sex change, and Glamour Man wears sunglasses.

SACRA VIA
(Looking around)
Hmmm, Damon Runyon died too soon.

GLAMOUR MAN
I am Glamour Man.

LADY GALAXY

You are horseshit.

SACRA VIA

Lady Galaxy, you are currently engaged in a most heated discussion . . . with horseshit.

GLAMOUR MAN

I'm bringing home the bacon. I am Glamour Man.

SACRA VIA

Oooh, the painted lady was last seen at the scene of the crime.

SAM

Crime!

NIGHTCLOUD

Lime!

SAM

Time! TIME! What we need is more time!

HEAVEN

The sands of time . . . the wind blew you farther away, like my vision of fresh-fallen dew.

LORD

What vision? Lay down!

DAPPER DARE

I was here first!

MARIE

I'm joining the line kids.

HEAVEN

The Ziegfeld Follies.

Everyone dances.

SACRA VIA

Princess Ninga Flinga Dung, you will sing again!

PRINCESS

(Chained, dragging her body around the floor)

I . . . I . . . will, Sacra Via? But—when will I walk again?

SACRA VIA

Only God can answer that, my child.

PRINCESS

(To God)

O God! O my God! Please, God! PLEASE!

HEAVEN

Little Miss Agnes Also-Ran.

SAM

Love conquers all.

HEAVEN

So does a good stiff drink of whiskey.

LADY GALAXY

Time waits for no man.

HEAVEN

Nightcloud, hurry—we must flee!

NIGHTCLOUD

I know a roadside diner.

HEAVEN

No more diners, please. No more hash houses or java joints! I'm through. If I have one more man, I shall burst as a poison boil!

LORD

You'll do as I say! Crystal Palace has left me this bordello in her will.
(Heaven laughs)
How quickly you laugh.

HEAVEN

She had no will. To live.

LORD

She left me this whore hole in her last will and testament.

HEAVEN

But she isn't dead yet!

References for this play:

Torch Song, starring Joan Crawford and Michael Wilding
The secret life of Adolf Hitler and Eva Braun
Spartacus, starring Kirk Douglas, Jean Simmons, Tony Curtis,
    Laurence Olivier, Peter Ustinov
The *Racing Form*
Aeschylus, *The Oresteian Trilogy*
TV GUIDE
Glamour, Glory, and Gold: The Life and Legend of Nola Noonan,
    Goddess and Star
Sheba, the greatest Queen of them all
All About Eve, starring Bette Davis, Anne Baxter, George Sanders,
    Gary Merrill, Celeste Holm, Marilyn Monroe, Thelma Ritter
Natalie Wood
Foster Grant sunglasses
ASCAP
A menu from Howard Johnson's
Shinola shoe dye
Gone with the Wind, starring Vivien Leigh, Clark Gable
The Ten Commandments
The Wizard of Oz, starring Judy Garland
Dick Tracy
Florenz Ziegfeld
Beverly Michaels
St. Vincent's Hospital
Dick Dale and the Deltones
Calamity Jane, a Doris Day starrer
De Carlo lots
Lady in the Dark, starring Ginger Rogers and Ray Milland
I Want to Live!, starring Susan Hayward

This list appeared at the end of Jackie's original script.

Craig Highberger

The reviews of *Heaven Grand in Amber Orbit* were laudatory. *Newsweek* called it "the wildest and in some ways the best show in New York," in particular singling out John Vaccaro's direction, and calling the performance "an explosion of pure theatrical energy unconfined by any effete ideas of form, content, structure or even rationality. It is an insanely intense, high-velocity, high-decibel circus, costume ball and scarifying super-ritual in which transvestism, scatology, obscenity, camp, self-assertion, self-depreciation, gallows humor, cloacal humor, sick humor, healthy humor, and cutting, soaring song all blast off through the tiny, backless-benched theater. The result is a theatrical purgative in which the company's maniac sincerity dissolves all the show's impurities into almost pure energy." Vaccaro later presented the play at Ellen Stewart's La Mama Experimental Theater Club in February 1970.

Holly Woodlawn

I was in Jackie's *Heaven Grand in Amber Orbit*, which was put on by John Vaccaro's Play-House of the Ridiculous. John Vaccaro actually fired Jackie from his own play. I was supposed to play Princess Ninga Flinga Dung, the Queen of Song. The character was supposed to have no arms and legs, and John Vaccaro directed me to crawl across the stage instead of walking. During rehearsal, I couldn't move fast enough and reach my mark on cue, and Vaccaro screamed at me, "Holly Woodlawn, you think you are a woman! You are a drag queen! You are no actress!" And finally the son of a bitch took my role. He played the Queen of Song and demoted me to the chorus. I was one of the Moon Reindeer Girls. So I decided to make as big a splash as I could in this little role, and I covered my entire body with Vaseline and glitter so I looked like a snake. I just wore a little fur-covered G-string, and I had nice little titties with fur pasties, and antlers, which were made of plastic leaves covered with glitter. I left a trail of glitter wherever I walked—when I went to the bathroom and flushed the toilet, it was full of glitter! So I did make my mark in the play, and Andy Warhol and Paul Morrissey came to see it, and I did an interview with *Gay Power* and said I was the new Warhol superstar, and they read it, and that's what led to me being cast in *Trash*. So it never would have happened without Curtis.

Ruby Lynn Reyner

Heaven Grand in Amber Orbit was a huge hit. Everyone came: underground stars, famous models, theater people from uptown. I remember James Rado and Gerome Ragni were there; this was when they were in the process of bringing *Hair* to Broadway. And I remember we'd go to these shows a year or two later and hear lines from Jackie's show, or see how they'd used his ideas.

Jackie and I lived together in an apartment for a few months. We had no money, so we stopped paying the rent and utilities. We went to Max's Kansas City every afternoon for happy hour because they served free hors d'oeuvres, and we would go and make a meal of the chicken wings or whatever they put out. I remember we woke up one afternoon and they had turned our electricity off. Jackie only had an electric shaver, so he couldn't shave, and we had to get over to the theater and he just put his makeup on over this heavy stubble and went and did the show like that.

Reverend Tim Holder

I remember being in study hall in the library of my high school one day and was reading *Newsweek* magazine because I was interested in politics. I turned the page and there was a theater review with the headline "Ridiculous," which turned out to be a very favorable review of Jackie Curtis's new play *Heaven Grand in Amber Orbit*. But, as they say, any kind of news can be good news, because here was a review of his play in a national magazine.

Paul Ambrose

I was from Tennessee originally. Thanks to *Playboy* magazine, I had heard of Jackie Curtis, Candy Darling, and Holly Woodlawn. I moved to Greenwich Village, and, after my nervous breakdown, I found that you could live on welfare and Medicaid. Medicaid would not only pay for you to go to the doctor; they would also pay for your medicine. So if you got medicines that other people would pay you for, you could make a hundred percent profit. I developed a reputation of being one of the few queens in the Village who would sell you real Tuinals that hadn't been cut. And Jackie Curtis occasionally needed a Tuinal, or another type of barbiturate, to come down from all the ups that he was taking. I was impressed as hell to meet Jackie.

Jackie was doing a show for John Vaccaro and the Play-House of the Ridiculous called *Cockstrong*. So I go to La Mama Experimental Theater Club and I see this twenty-foot-long cock that stands during the entire play, and then falls forward at the end of it and shoots white liquid out onto everyone in the audience. I mean, I had just come from Tennessee a year before, and from preaching. Granted, I was no longer preaching, but I was surprised. During the play, Jackie Curtis came out at one point. It really was a defining moment in my life, because, until then, I had never seen a great star live on stage. Jackie comes out in this black outfit with this red frizzed hair and glitter and black eye shadow and ripped stockings and sang the "Fucking-A Douche Bag Blues," and I had never seen anything like it in my life. And, to this day, it ranks with Ethel Merman and Carol Channing; I mean, really, as good as anything I have seen on Broadway. As good as Barbara Cook, or Bernadette Peters, or anyone who is considered to be great. Jackie could match them on the good nights. A friend was in the show, and I made him introduce me to Jackie backstage, and we became friendly.

Styles Caldwell

In 1969, I lived in New York, and I was fascinated by what was going on in underground film and theater. And one very hot summer day, I was walking down Fourth Street and I walked past La Mama and all the doors were opened, and I looked in there and a show was going on, and it was a Play-House of the Ridiculous production, directed by John Vaccaro, called *Cockstrong*, and they said come on in and see the show. And it was in the middle of the show—and there was Jackie Curtis, singing a song called "Talking Dirty to the One You Love." And I'll never forget the finale was a gigantic cock that fell forward toward the audience and sprayed everybody with white liquid—unbelievable! I was in heaven. So I came back the next night and saw the whole show, and afterward I went backstage and I went up to Jackie and I said, "You were absolutely wonderful!" And he was really friendly. And I started seeing Jackie at night in the West Village, walking around in a dress, looking very glamorous, with Rita Redd or Candy Darling.

Penny Arcade

Our world, the Lower East Side downtown art scene, was filled with wildly talented people. There was an awareness of sadness. There was never any question that there were enormous wounds. But it was, like, let's put on a show to cover up all of this despair and misery. Our lives were bleak, so we filled them with glitter.

Jackie's play *Femme Fatale* was based on Jackie, me, and our real-life adventures. We had a quintessential fag/fag hag relationship. The play was also about John Christian, who, at the age of eighteen, became Diana Ross and the Supremes' hairdresser. But John became a junkie and agoraphobic and died of cirrhosis. Patti Smith played the John Christian role.

I had had a falling out with John Vaccaro, of the Play-House of the Ridiculous, who was an immense influence on Jackie. John was furious when I told him I was going to appear in *Femme Fatale*, and said, "You're out, YOU ARE OUT!" Because of that, I did the entire play as John Vaccaro, using his voice. My role was Poo-Poo Cushman, and it was an inside joke making fun of John. Obviously, I wasn't much of a careerist. I was more intent upon amusing Jackie. I got a lot of attention and good reviews during the run of *Femme Fatale,* and Jackie got very upset about it. And one of the most harrowing betrayals of my life was when Jackie became angry that I was getting as much attention as he was. And we didn't speak for about three years after that.

Paul Ambrose

Blanche Emerson used to call Jackie the "Oatmeal Woman," because Jackie would paint his face and then it would cake, and then he would paint over that and cake, and paint and cake— until the surface was literally an oatmeal texture. I don't know what he saw in the mirror but it was not that rough oatmeal texture. Whatever he saw, he thought that he actually could get a job looking like that, or, at the very least, be interviewed on television. Jackie would go out into the streets in this bright orange, crackled oatmeal makeup, with his hair tied up in a turban made of torn nylon stockings, and an army jacket, and black torn tights. This is the way he was dressed in the fall of 1970, when he went to the auditions for the Broadway musical *No, No, Nanette.*

Jackie and Candy Darling and I went to audition together. I

was going under the theory that if they just saw me, maybe I'd get a part. That was my only hope, because I knew that I could not dance. Candy Darling said, in her breathy, Kim Novak stage whisper, when we arrived, "I'm here for a part—I'm here for Flora from Frisco." And she refused to do anything except walk across the stage and sit down in front and wait for Busby Berkeley to arrive. I wore a very tasteful blue kimono from the twenties, with a giant rhinestone pin holding it together at the side, a big ostrich feather boa, a big blue lace hat, and big blue sunglasses, black tights with a black leotard underneath, and a cupid-bow mouth, period makeup.

Jackie goes on in the group before me, and I'm standing next to the dance directors, and they're the ones who were actually doing the casting—Busby Berkeley was just part of it for the name value. So I hear one of these dance directors say to the other, "Should we give this tired drag queen a chance?" Jackie could dance, and they had the girls do the time step, and then they called, "Next group." I had been practicing all day and I could not dance. I knew my only hope was to make an impression, so I went out to center stage, and first I took the boa—fling, into the wings; then the hat—into the wings; the glasses—into the wings. I [took] the pin, removed it from my hip, and the kimono shimmied down to the floor, leaving me in a leotard holding this rhinestone pin above my head. There was nothing but stunned silence. Then, from the wings, I hear, "You, dear. Yes, you. You're too tall."

Robert Heide

Jackie was a real dame—in the Busby Berkeley sense of it. I was there when Jackie and Candy and Marie auditioned for the musical *No, No, Nanette*. Jackie didn't look very good in those days. Jackie liked to drink in those Lower East Side holes and was always recovering from some bender. At the auditions, I remember

Candy Darling was glowing in a 1930s outfit. I think Jackie was just kind of hanging out. I do remember Busby giving Jackie a kind of dirty look at one point, because he didn't think he was right for the chorus. But I don't think Busby had any idea of what was really going on that day.

Jackie to me always was kind of a sad, glad rag doll, ragamuffin, street urchin, a stoop sitter. Jackie was everywhere; she wasn't holed up somewhere, as Candy might be, in a fancy restaurant—Bleecker or Beekman Towers, or that sort of thing. I think of Jackie as very hard-edged, but also very angelic; there was a kind of, just behind the façade, the confused boy, the kind of charm that could sometimes stab you—with a knife. Also, in talking with Jackie, there was a wonderful kind of empathy, not pretentious. I mean, Candy was Carole Lombard, and Jackie was more the B-girl, the Barbara Stanwyck or Gloria Grahame type, the Novocaine lips covered with glitter. Lisabeth Scott, there's a little of that too. I can hear Jackie saying one of my favorite Lizabeth Scott lines: "It's not that I was old. . . . It's just that I wasn't . . . young anymore."

CHAPTER 5

Warhol and the Underground Movies

Jackie Curtis running through a scene with director Paul Morrissey
and cameraman Andy Warhol during the filming of *Women in Revolt* in 1971.
(Photo by Gretchen Berg)

Andy Warhol

Jackie Curtis isn't a drag queen; Jackie is an artist, a pioneer without a frontier.

Excerpt from Jackie's journal, 1972:

Some people are born to run. Some people are born to rule. Some people are born to play pinball. Some people are born to be blond. Some people are born to lose. While others are born to be wild. Bad, wicked, and wild. Everybody gets to know them real well. Me? I was lucky just to be born at all. Plus I read somewhere in a very old first-edition lime green almanac, that being born on February nineteenth is the hardest star in the constellation to place.

I was definitely born too late. Nobody told me that by the time I got out of school there would be no more studio system. Well, what could I do? I go to the gates and yell, "Jonesey!" Gone are those lush days, when a star could disappear for two weeks on a whim, and not show up and hold up production. The front office just couldn't handle it anymore, even if your pictures weren't slipping at the box office. No more Doris Day, no more Judy Garland, no more Gary Cooper, no more June Allison. The grooming of the new talent would now become the grooming of the no-talents. It was something akin to the night before Christmas—not a creature was stirring, not even Mickey Mouse. Nothing, no lights, no camera—no action.

Remember, it's Andy Warhol who became a silver-haired shaman, or a father, if you will—of the sixties. He brought not just films to the screen, not just stars, but superstars. Don't you get tired with all these movies today about junkies, and drug addicts, and dope fiends. If we have to have movies like that, why can't they all be musicals? I have just written a script for the world's first dope musical. It opens in a luxury penthouse on Mott Street with our heroine—that's the leading lady—pacing the living-room floor. She's nervously biting her fingers and her toes. She goes to the window, throws it open, and says, "What's taking Frenchy so long? Why doesn't he come? And bring me that which I must have. Take away your kisses and your hugs, but don't take away my dangerous drugs."

Craig Highberger

There are several versions of how Warhol and Curtis first met. According to an interview that Jackie Curtis gave to Patrick Smith, for the book *Andy Warhol's Art and Films*, Jackie first met Andy Warhol in 1965, on Forty-seventh Street and Second Avenue, when he was staying at the YMCA across the street from the silver Factory.

The other version is Andy Warhol's recollection. He remembered first meeting Jackie Curtis and Candy Darling in 1966 while walking through Greenwich Village with Fred Hughes, on his way to pick up a pair of leather pants at the Leather Man.

Jackie was about nineteen, tall and gangly with a Beatles mop-top haircut. Walking with him was a tall, sensational, blond drag queen in high heels and a sundress with one strap falling onto her upper arm. Jackie introduced the blonde as Hope Slattery, the name Candy was using in those days; her real name was Jimmy Slattery.

Jackie recognized Warhol immediately, and asked for his autograph on the shopping bag he was carrying. When Andy asked what was is in the bag, Jackie pulled out several pairs of red satin shorts and told him they were for the tap-dancing scene in his new play, *Glamour, Glory, and Gold.* Curtis promised to send Warhol tickets to the opening-night performance.

Joe Dallesandro

After doing *Loves of Ondine* and *Lonesome Cowboys* for Warhol and Morrissey, I thought they were the silliest things I had ever seen. I couldn't believe that they were real movies. So when Paul Morrissey called me up again he kept saying, "We do real movies—we do real movies." Paul's idea of directing was telling us what he wanted the action in the scene to be about and the way he wanted the story to go, and have us improvise dialogue around what he had just told us.

The scene I did with Jackie Curtis, Candy Darling, and Geri Miller in *Flesh*: Geri played a topless go-go dancer who was trying to impress me with her breasts. The Jackie Curtis I had met for *Flesh* was really horrible-looking, because he didn't look right dressed as a woman. He looked like a man dressed as a woman, and it was just—not right. Candy and Jackie sat on a couch and read movie magazines as I had this go-go dancer doing titty dances in front of me, trying to arouse me.

The *Flesh* story line concerned a guy waking up with his so-called wife and having to go out and hustle because his wife's girlfriend needs an abortion. We called them "Underground Movies" because they were done without crews, with non-actors, shot very quickly on 16-millimeter film. The film had a big success. Success is if people show up and buy tickets. They had an audience. I was pretty amazed, because I couldn't sit and watch them. Paul came up with the idea of having some people call the police and complain that *Flesh* was obscene, so that it would be shut down for some legal bullshit for a day. He'd have these plants go in and do this, but, because the censor was a big fan of mine, they wouldn't force us to cut it, and the next day they could show the film again. It was just to get all this publicity and coverage, and it worked.

Audience members and critics thought of them in the beginning as documentaries. So I went with that. It used to piss Paul off, because I heard them say that these films were telling our real stories, and I thought, Go with it, play it—but it used to make Paul crazy that I would say that shit.

We took *Flesh* to film festivals, and we went to Italy, and I remember we were talking to these distributors in Rome, and this one said, "You know, it doesn't make sense for us to take this film, because we don't have this kind of problem here. Nobody would relate." And I said, But I thought prostitution was the oldest profession, I thought it came out of Rome—what are you telling me, that there is absolutely no male prostitution in Italy? And he said, "No, nobody would understand that."

I always treated Jackie and Holly and Candy very nice, because I always felt that it is hard enough just wanting to be an actor or an actress. What roles can these people do? They can only play a person in drag. Even in Candy's case, and Candy was beautiful—it still was a man. I could never think of Candy as a real woman. But they were nice people, and they had their dreams and fantasies. For the moment that I had to be with them, why should I burst their bubble? They were women for that moment.

Paul Morrissey

What I liked about Jackie was what I liked about Holly later, the fact that there was nothing feminine about Jackie. He made no attempt to act in a feminine way. The makeup he wore didn't go far to make him look feminine either. During that time, I had run into Candy Darling a few places, and she was entirely feminine, which was great. And they made a good contrast. We shot their scene for

Flesh in my office, right there on Union Square, just in front of my desk. If you look at the film, you can tell they are both kind of nervous. And they both look very unkempt, because they had no money to have good makeup or hair, and, in the movie, Candy Darling talks about the fact that her hair looks awful.

It wasn't the study of acting that made them interesting. Either they are born with something inherently interesting, like Jackie and Candy and Holly, or they're not. And they're not going to learn that in their awful acting classes. All people learn in acting classes is how to scream and yell and behave like the lowest class of people you wouldn't want to be around. I don't know why they keep putting people like that in movies, but they do.

Jackie

Being a Warhol superstar, I was invited to a lot of parties, and those I wasn't invited to I could crash. And at these parties I met an awful lot of people with money, which is very important in a commercial industry like show business. It opened many doors for me, and it was one of the richest learning experiences in my life. Things I would never have looked up in books, dictionaries, chemistry reference books, used-car records; I tried to delve into areas I had never been interested in before. And even though I couldn't quote a thing now, at the time it gave me many avenues to escape from just being fabulous on the outside. I wanted to be able to converse with people; I didn't just want to say things like, "Isn't Lana Turner wonderful?" You know, I didn't want to just be a joke. I never wanted to be a queen with subjects.

Holly Woodlawn

There was a major incident where I wound up in jail. It was 1970, and I had a friend who was apartment sitting at this fabulous place near the United Nations. It was the apartment of the French ambassador to the U.N. He was traveling, and my friend had the place for several weeks. I stayed with him in this divine luxury, and, of course, I couldn't help trying on the wife's dresses and things. And while I was peeking into drawers, we found her passport and her checkbook. I had some photo proof sheet from a Jack Mitchell shoot, and one of the shots was just the right size. I cut it out and we taped over it so it looked like it was laminated to the passport. So my friend and I went to the bank, and I had made out a check for two thousand dollars and used the fake passport, and we got away with two thousand dollars! Of course, after a few days that was gone, so we stupidly went back and tried it again, and they nabbed me. I spent a month in jail.

In *Variety*, there was a banner headline: TRASH STAR FOUND IN TRASHCAN. The warden come up to me and said, "Oh, is this you?," and there is a photo of me in the Sunday *New York Times,* reviewing the film, saying Holly Woodlawn is fabulous in *Trash.* Later that day, he says you are now out on bail, and I said, Who has paid my bail? It was the artist Larry Rivers. I called him right up to thank him, and he said, Come on over, Jackie Curtis is here; she called me up, and said, "You gotta get Holly out of jail." If it hadn't been for Jackie, I would have been in jail for God knows how long. Andy Warhol didn't come to my rescue. My parents didn't even come to my rescue. Jackie called up everyone, and said, You can't let Holly rot in jail. Her movie's just opened.

Jackie said, Larry and I are going to take you out to see *Trash* tonight, and I have alerted the media, there are going to be photographers and reporters there. That sounded wonderful, but I was an absolute mess because I had been in jail for thirty days. So Larry, angel that he was, took us to Bloomingdale's, and said, "Girls, go shopping," and we did. I got my hair done, and Jackie and I went through all the dresses, and I got this fabulous dress and Jackie got a fabulous housedress. We go back to Larry's to get ready for the limousine ride to the theater. What does Curtis do? She just rips the shit out of her brand-new dress so it looks like a tattered rag! Then she takes her new stockings and just tears them to shreds. I said, "Jackie, what are you doing?" She goes, "It's a look, isn't it?"

Laura de Coppet

Jackie needed benefactors, and he did find them. And Leo Castelli was one, because he was touched by Jackie. I was a great benefactor of Jackie's, and in Andy Warhol's diaries Andy says, "I can't believe that this is the girl that is giving Jackie Curtis money for drugs!"

Jackie

The first thing Andy Warhol said to me was, "Do you want to be a star? You won't have to do anything for it." In my head, I wanted to do everything. I wanted to sing, dance, talk, be a man, be a woman, and wear furs. Andy and I were very close while we worked on *Women in Revolt*, but he didn't take me to parties. He took Candy and Holly, because they were girls. I felt like Medusa, unable to go out in public. I felt I was being abandoned, when I was his biggest star. I realized later that he was right. I wasn't a "party girl"; I was a method actor. I was a "superstar." I showed everyone you could change your sex, you could be male or female, without surgery.

Paul Morrissey

Women in Revolt was meant to be a leading part for Holly. The idea of her being a women's libber was my amusing take on this idea that was just starting then, that women should be just like men. It was a silly idea, it's been proven, but it's not going to stop.

It seemed to me a funny idea, a comical idea, that men who had devoted their lives to assuming the roles of women should be asked to play women who had been told by the women's liberation movement that they should assume the roles of men. So I mentioned it to Andy Warhol. I said, I think they should play women's libbers. Like that ridiculous Valerie Solanas, who had shot him a few years before. Andy was very brave about it. He said, "That's a good idea." I don't remember ever saying to Andy anything that he didn't say was a good idea. Warhol was so glad to have any ideas, because he didn't come up with any himself, I remember. He wasn't the kind of person who had funny ideas or creative ideas.

I remember after *Women in Revolt* was released reading an interview with Jackie where she said, "I like it when Andy directs me, not Paul." Andy never directed anybody. What she liked was, Andy didn't interfere with her. Andy didn't interfere with anybody, because he didn't know what to interfere with.

Jackie dominates the movie with this strong character Jackie had. The remarks she makes are funny in a Jackie way, while the remarks Candy makes are funny in a Candy Darling way. You become very sympathetic to the plight of women. And you sort of say to yourself, Gee, it isn't easy being a woman. You wouldn't say that if women were playing the parts, you'd just take it for granted. But because the roles are being played by men, because men are going through these problems pretending to be women, I think it makes it much more effective.

I operated with Jackie and Candy in *Women in Revolt* the same as in every film that I've made: without a script. I would always just explain to Jackie very briefly. I would say, "Jackie, in this scene this is the guy you're trying to pay to have sex with. He is Mr. America; you are a women's libber." I would give them each the basis of the scene, and I would suggest lines, and then we would just turn on the camera. What I think this did, in retrospect, is it took out self-consciousness, and it made them just take chances.

These films, besides being unusual when you see them—no films in the history of the world ever were made in this way, where they were actually made in ten hours on afternoons. It always disappointed me that these pioneer female impersonators were so gifted and so funny and yet had such a hard time making any money—if they made any at all. They lived very difficult lives.

Harvey Fierstein

Jackie could look beautiful. And Jackie could look very real. I think in *Women in Revolt* there are some scenes where Jackie looks very real. I don't know what went on in his mind when he would go outside unshaven wearing lipstick. But it was almost like, I don't want to look like anybody else. I want to do this my way.

Jack Mitchell

In the fall of 1970, I went over to an apartment that Paul Morrissey and Andy Warhol were using to film a scene of their new movie, *Women in Revolt*. I took photographs between camera setups. Jackie was performing in the scene with a baby. When she walked into the studio, she was wearing kind of a suburban housewife outfit—just a simple housedress, and very plain makeup.

Of the three Warhol transvestite stars—Jackie, Holly, and Candy—Jackie Curtis was by far the most cerebral. She was a no-nonsense and motivated person—sort of like Rosalind Russell doing a Paddy Chayefsky play, one of those kitchen-sink dramas he was famous for in the fifties. I could see Jackie doing the Marjorie Main role in *The Women*. What a pity they couldn't have cast Jackie in that role for the Broadway stage version; he would have been a great success.

Holly Woodlawn

One of my favorite moments working with Jackie was making *Women in Revolt*, with Andy Warhol and Paul Morrissey. We shot it in maybe ten days over a period of a couple of months. At the end of every day's shooting, we would sign the release form, and they would pay us twenty-five dollars, which we were happy with. We were "superstars," and got a lot of attention at Max's Kansas City. So the film had been out for some time and had a lot of attention and big audiences. So Jackie devised this plan. He said, Why don't we go to Max's for dinner, and order filet mignon and lobster and wine, and sign Andy Warhol's name? So we did this for about a month before Andy found out and the jig was up.

Harvey Fierstein

I couldn't believe that we would all go to Max's Kansas City, sit at Warhol's table in the back, and eat and drink, and then walk out on the check. But Jackie said it was all right to do, so we did it. Jackie would do that all the time.

Gretchen Berg

Jackie and I drifted apart for several years, I think because I had taken a job with the *New York Free Press*, and I became very involved with the anti–Vietnam War movement, which wasn't something Jackie was interested in. We met again in 1971, when I was working for *Show* magazine, a now-defunct entertainment publication funded by Huntington Hartford. I went to do an interview and take photographs during the filming of Paul Morrissey's *Women in Revolt*. Jackie was no longer the redheaded kid with the Beatle haircut. He was twenty-three, and he had a new drag persona. He was very edgy, almost nervous. I found it very difficult to talk to Jackie. It was as if he had withdrawn behind the mirror, behind panes of glass—farther and farther away.

Jackie still loved to have his picture taken, but I could see that the person I had known was now submerged—not really there anymore. It's like when you send a child to boarding school for the first time and you go to meet them, the child that comes across the grass to you is not the same child. The famous fakir trick, with the little boy or little girl inside the straw basket into which swords are plunged, and then the top is taken off and the child jumps out—that is not the same child. Jackie was not the same person. He was engrossed in becoming the person, the woman, in that film, and I watched him step into the mirror, into the camera, and become that persona. Very, very seldom did I see even a glimmer of the old Jackie.

Holly Woodlawn

So one afternoon we went over to the Factory to visit Andy. Really, we arrived unannounced like this because we were there to hit him up for some money, which we had done before. But Pat Hackett, who was the secretary, stopped us, and said that Andy wasn't there. There was a nice reception area with some chairs, so we said we'd just wait, but she said he had called and said he wasn't coming in. So we went across the street to the park in Irving Place, and, sure enough, in less than an hour, there came a taxi and Andy got out and we saw him go upstairs. So we went back into the building and down into the basement, and we found the power panel. It was unlocked, and everything was labeled, and so we shut off every breaker for Andy's floor. Then we went upstairs in the elevator, and when the door opened we screamed into the dark space, "Andy Warhol, you are dead! We know how to use a gun!," and made our exit. The next day, our rent was paid.

Jackie

Working with Andy Warhol and being part of his inner circle was like walking into a desert of destroyed egos. It was like being in the cold room where they work with dangerous flammable chemicals, where everything is twenty degrees below zero. You've got to have incredible stamina and drive to hang out with them. I was the black sheep of the Warhol crowd. I was definitely not the darling. Candy was the darling. I was the rebel. I could tell from the way I was treated that I was certainly not a welcome addition. But I was one of their hottest properties at the time, and I knew it. And I knew what I could demand, just as Greta Garbo did when she was at M-G-M. Greta Garbo demanded the highest salary, and Louis B. Mayer said no, and she would just say, "I think I go home," turn on her heel, and leave. That's what I did, and we got along very well after that.

Michael Musto

Jackie was obsessed with stardom, the Hollywood system, the glamour machine, and he ended up part of it, in a way, because he was a Warhol superstar. Jackie told me that he survived the Warhol years because he was already Jackie Curtis before he met Andy, so she could still be Jackie Curtis afterward. The wonderful thing is that he became a star. Whether it was a Warhol superstar, or just a stage star. He never got to be the movie star that he no doubt envisioned himself as, but he did fashion himself, when he was younger, [as] a combination of Audrey Hepburn and Jean Seberg. He was obsessed with the Hollywood glitter machine, and I'm sure Jackie had glitter in his veins instead of blood.

He deserved a star on the [Hollywood] Walk of Fame, because he was a star. Even if he was living out of a shoebox, eking out a living doing stage work off-off-off-Broadway. Still, he was the biggest Hollywood star in his mind, and in my mind.

And it was just so sweet to see him living a dream, even on a shoebox level. And working in themes of fame and glamour, that's what all his shows were about. They were all about the star-making process, and he was obsessed with larger-than-life divas, and glamorous icons—and, in the process of playing them, he became one.

Laura de Coppet

When I finished my book on the art dealers, I called different people to ask them to give quotes for the dust jacket, and one of the people I called was Andy Warhol. But Andy said, I don't really have anything to say, why don't you get someone to come up with something clever and just put my name to it. And I said, Really?, and he said, That's fine. And I said, Well, Jackie Curtis is here. Andy said, "Perfect, have him do it." I put the phone down, and said, Curtis, he wants you to do his quote. He said, "Oh ducky, how perfect. We'll start with 'Gee': 'Gee, it's all here—the truth behind the art, the art behind the truth. A book for grown-ups about the art world—Andy Warhol." And everybody thinks it's Andy Warhol's quote. But it isn't—it's Jackie Curtis's.

CHAPTER 6

Vain Victory

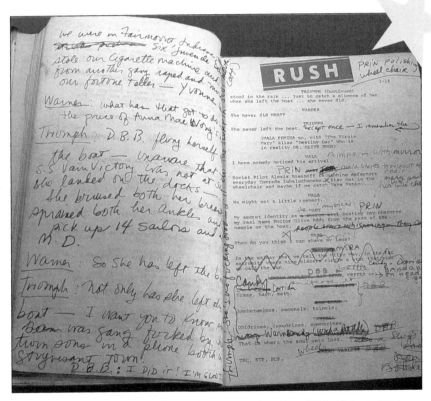

Fueled by drug use, Jackie's heavily annotated script of *Vain Victory*, 1971.
Some pages exhibit multiple superimposed layers of writing in different colors.
(The Estate of Jackie Curtis)

Paul Serrato

Around 1970, Jackie had the backing and the resources to do a new musical, and that one was going to be called *Vain Victory*. This was around the time that *Hair* had opened uptown on Broadway, and we were going to do *Vain Victory* downtown, where a lot of the artistic, innovative, alternative culture was really happening—below Fourteenth Street. *Vain Victory* was produced at Ellen Stewart's La Mama Theater, on East Fourth Street. Every counterculture star that you can name was in it.

Jackie, of course, was friends with all artists; everybody loved him, and wanted to help this young kid from the Lower East Side see his projects through. The scenery for *Vain Victory* included beautiful hanging clouds created by Larry Rivers. Andy Warhol donated a big silkscreen of one of his cows. The music was provided not only by myself but also by Peter Allen, who wrote some tunes for it, and Eric Emerson, who wrote and performed a couple of the tunes. The show opened at La Mama, and it became an immediate smash hit.

When we were doing *Vain Victory*, the persona he was projecting was that of James Dean. Jackie was so into the James Dean myth that the set for *Vain Victory* included the shell of a car, which became the focal point of a lot of the singing and a lot of the action. That was because James Dean died in a car crash. About a year or so later, when *Grease* opened on Broadway, there was a car on stage as part of the set. This is another instance where uptown would come downtown and look around, to check out all the creative ideas, to see what they could pick up and use and take uptown and make money on and let it go mainstream.

Some nights, twenty or thirty people got up out of the audience, including Andy Warhol, and took part in the production. The show was only supposed to have a two-week run, but it was so successful that it ran the entire summer of 1971. I think of *Vain Victory* as the downtown answer to *Hair*, because *Hair* was a countercultural hit for the mainstream audiences uptown, and downtown you had *Vain Victory*, which was the countercultural statement of people who really were involved with the counterculture, who were the counterculture.

Several scenes of *Vain Victory* were filmed by PBS and incorporated into the series called *An American Family*. In the second episode, Lance Loud's mother comes to the Chelsea Hotel, where Lance is struggling with coming out. Lance decides to take her to La Mama to see *Vain Victory*. The show included a wonderful moment when Jackie walks down an immense staircase singing. He performed as Blue Denim, the male lead in the show. Candy Darling was the female star, and performed the role of Donna Bella Beads, in a mermaid outfit.

Paul Ambrose

Through Jackie I met the director Anthony Ingrassia, who thought I was perfect to play the part of Mother Cabrini in a play. I freaked out, because I have never been any good at standing up in front of audiences. I always get terrible stage fright. I couldn't even read out loud in school. That's why it is so ironic that I ended up trying to be an actor. I declined the part of Mother Cabrini. But then Jackie started talking about her next play. She said it was going to be something called *Vain Victory: The Vicissitudes of the Damned*. She wanted me for the part of Juicy Lucy, and we went uptown to some fabulous place on Central Park West that was supposed to be Barbra Streisand's apartment. We walked in, and there were all these society people, art patrons, and gallery owners—all there for this reading of Jackie's play. That was my first public appearance as Juicy Lucy. "My name is Juicy Lucy, I'm a water baby, my skin screams to remain moist." I had long blond hair, you know, a hundred pounds ago. I thought I was in show business. I was so naive; I had no idea that if you did a show in drag that you were likely to be considered a woman for the rest of your life. For years, people would only treat me nicely if I answered to the name Marie. This is Jackie Curtis's doing.

Juicy Lucy got to be a bigger part as rehearsals went on. There was some talk about it being my fault, because I could handle more drugs than most of them, and I would get them real high and then take their lines. I swear I didn't do this on purpose, but there was talk.

The rehearsals for *Vain Victory* lasted for six months. They were over at the La Mama loft, and the first thing Jackie did was paint the window glass black so no light came in at all. Jackie decided to direct this one himself. He had just started shooting speed, and things were a little odd at times. To rehearse more than a week or two was unheard of, because, typically, a show only ran two weekends. Ellen Stewart was just wonderful, and she supported six months of rehearsals. During all that time, we never ever [went] through the entire play in one evening. There'd be a twelve-hour shift of one group, and then some of them would sleep in the back and some of them would crawl home. Whoever was there was the scene we did. We were sort of like the circus in town, and everyone would come to the *Vain Victory* rehearsals, because, day and night, they were running because Jackie kept us high. Lily Tomlin was there with Jane Wagner. Gary Cooper's daughter was there. And Sandy Dennis, who just loved Jackie. Somewhere along the line— and I'm not saying there's anything wrong with this—Bette Midler saw Candy Darling in a mermaid outfit, and me in a wheelchair, and ended up on stage a year later in a wheelchair wearing a mermaid outfit.

Agosto Machado

In 1970, my neighbor across the hall was the very handsome young actor Robert La Tourneaux, who had just starred as Cowboy, the hustler, Harold's birthday present in the fabulous motion picture of *Boys in the Band*. Robert really was a hunk, and Jackie Curtis adored him, and was kind of stalking him, coming by to visit and trying to persuade him to be in his next show, *Vain Victory*. I was very thrilled to be Robert's neighbor and friend, and I was delighted to run into Jackie Curtis one day, who was standing outside Robert's door writing him a note because he wasn't at home. I was so thrilled to see Jackie Curtis that I was speechless—I think I mumbled hello as I walked slowly to my door and unlocked it and went inside, never taking my eyes off of her.

To my delight, a minute later she knocked on my door! I opened the door and gave her a big smile and said, "Yes?," and she said, "Can you sing?" I was crestfallen and said no. She said, "Well, can you dance?" And I said no. She said, "Can you act?" And I said no. And she said, "Do you want to be in a show?" And I said, YES!!!

And I always say, opportunity didn't knock on my door—Jackie Curtis did.

Lily Tomlin

When I met Jane Wagner, one of the first things she said to me was, You have to meet Jackie Curtis; you have to see what he's doing and the kind of things he represents. And so we went to see *Vain Victory*, which was in rehearsals at La Mama, and I feel really privileged that I was part of that whole society, even in a peripheral way. Before it opened, Jane and I had to go back to California, so on opening night we sent him a telegram congratulating him and wishing him great success.

Styles Caldwell

Being in *Vain Victory* was the most exciting time of my life. All of these fabulous people were in it. Eric Emerson was one of the stars. . . . He was so cute and nice. He was coming on to everybody. He had about five illegitimate children and a hundred boyfriends. He was very busy. I used to see him going down Christopher Street. Eric took ballet classes, and he'd do these leaps and pirouettes down the street wearing only a pair of cutoffs in the summer. He had an incredible body. No wonder Jackie Curtis wanted to get married to him the summer of 1969.

Paul Ambrose

Jackie took me in after I was arrested for murder. I discovered there are two kinds of people in the world: [the ones who asked] Who did you kill?, or, Did you do it? Jackie was one of the "Did you do it?" people, and when I was released, because I did not do it, my friends were crossing the street to avoid me. Jackie took me into his house and made everyone accept me socially, because if you wanted to see Jackie I was with him. He took me to the Factory, and Holly Woodlawn greeted me with open arms and called me "dear sister," because she had just gotten out too, after the French ambassador's wife's affair.

Paul Morrissey claims not to remember that around that time he greeted me by saying, "You think you could play a man in our new movie? It's a western." Well, yes, Paul, I think I could play a man. Because I *am* a man. "You think you could play a murderer?" I said, "Yes, Paul. I suppose you've heard I've been practicing." He swears the conversation did not happen, but I remember it clearly. They never did the movie, and I never got a part. Shortly thereafter, Jackie cast me in *Vain Victory*. Whatever career I have had, it's all due to Jackie Curtis, because nobody would acknowledge me until Jackie made them acknowledge me. And Jackie gave me every opportunity to shine in the play. Everybody in *Vain Victory*, out of a cast of more than twenty, had their moment, and Jackie made sure it was played up. Jackie was not going to give an inch when he was on stage, but was generous enough to give you your moment—if you could take it from Jackie. If Jackie wasn't on stage, you were home free. If he was, you had your chance if you could take it.

Craig Highberger

Jackie wrote *Vain Victory: The Vicissitudes of the Damned* between 1969 and 1971. Ellen Stewart, founder of La Mama Experimental Theater Club, put it on the 1971 schedule, and supported an unprecedented six months of rehearsals. Jackie's rehearsal copy of the script is more than one inch thick—more than two hundred pages—with scene deletions and copious additions, new dialogue, setting descriptions, costume notes, and sketches on the back of nearly every single page. Jackie was almost constantly on speed during this period, according to many sources. The show, when it opened, ran two and a half hours, after trimming it a full one third.

The script was set alternately at a high school graduation, a circus, in Hollywood, and on board the good ship *Vain Victory*. The characters included leading men Dorrian Gray and Eric Emerson, who played a combination angel/cowboy. Styles Caldwell, who was also a member of the cast, remembers that before every performance they slathered Eric's naked body with Vaseline and then covered his entire body with silver glitter, except for his penis— which was covered in bright red glitter! Emerson's costume consisted of a pair of leather chaps (bottomless and crotchless) and a cowboy hat! At some point during the first week of the play, Jackie and Eric were convinced to cover Eric's charms to avoid the very real possibility of the police closing the play for public obscenity.

The show became an instant smash hit. Andy Warhol came

opening night, and to numerous other performances, with an entourage, because Jackie had advertised that Warhol was a cast member; he was billed as "The Winged Avenger." During the show, he stood up and took pictures with his Polaroid SX-70 camera. Ellen Stewart remembers that opening night Jackie came out to talk to Andy during intermission, and told the audience that he was ghostwriter for the show!

One evening, less than a half hour before curtain, a frantic call came to the box office. The audience was informed that the show would be starting late, because John Lennon, Yoko Ono, and their party, who had reserved the entire front row, were running late at an uptown restaurant.

The successful run was extended as long as possible at La Mama and then moved to another venue—the WPA Theater, on the Bowery—for another eight weeks. The show ran for a total of six months.

VAIN VICTORY: THE VICISSITUDES OF THE DAMNED
A comedy by
JACKIE CURTIS

Cast of Characters
Triumph Avenue, the Great Impresario
Caminada Phantom, a cowboy, the Man in the
Moon
Cream Varlett, a cowboy on the run and a juvenile
delinquent
Big Bead, a cowboy on the run and a juvenile
delinquent
Wheels, a cowboy on the run and a juvenile
delinquent
The House of Wax Girls, the chorines
Madame Bertha, the head of the House of Wax

Canta Lupe, a Spanish vocalist and maid to
Donna Bella Beads
Career Kit, an agent who books variety acts
Esta Nil, a featured guest vocalist with the House
of Wax
Mary, the Virgin Mary
Madonna, leader of the first and original "Cult of
Evil" of the Carnival World
Mala Femina, a wheelchair-ridden aerialist
Dura, as in Durable, the fire swallower
Ha-Ha, prince of the high wire, son of Donna
Bella Beads
Gray Idiot, prince of the high wire, son of Donna
Bella Beads
Pappa Razzi, a detective posing as an Italian
monsignor
Elmsford Hastings, a lost safari member, Bravado,
the Comanche warrior
Mira-Mira!, the black queen of the City of Night
and debutante Mona Kimball Ward
Warner Color, an ambitious young man, Soviet
pilot Alexis Rosanoff
Donna Bella Beads, queen of the high wire, who
was Vana Venko in a former life
Christian Faith, member of the original
"Cult of Evil"
Anna Sin, member of the original "Cult of Evil"
Paramount, from the Foreign Legion, disguised as
Clark Kent
Major Cyclonica, the great mynah bird
Vice Versa, the ship's captain, Via Crucis, the
winged avenger
Benito Bustello, a little prince

Abolena Bustello, twin sister to Benito; she is
princess of Arabia
Fatima Velasquez, the veiled wanderer
Juicy Lucy and Big Bust, the starlets of Pig Alley,
the girls from Chorine Beach

Excerpt from Act II—the lifeboat.

CAMINADA
I know how one can suffer those first evenings
on the high seas. While one's soul is still a
stranger. Do I sleep? you ask yourself. Do I wait up
for dawn? Will the others?

TRIUMPH
What have you asked of nature?

BIG BEAD
You said it wouldn't rain . . . it's very cloudy.

CREAM VARLETT
It's not entirely impossible we might drown out
here.

TRIUMPH
To the highest attractive energy man gave the
name of divine. For its control he invested the sci-
ence called religion, a word which then meant and
still means the cultivation of occult forces.

BIG BUST
I have no friends. Just Christmas balls and pep-
permint sticks.

MADONNA

Paramount! Leave her be, she's a long way from home.

PARAMOUNT

She almost went under for the third time.

CHRISTIAN FAITH

He who dances, lives. He who sings, speaks truth. He who closes his eyes, sleeps.

ANNA SIN

Those who voluntarily put power into the hands of a tyrant or enemy must not wonder if it might at last be turned against themselves.

TRIUMPH

Faster, you fools! Faster!

PARAMOUNT

Listen! A buoy!

TRIUMPH

What impious mortal bent on death draws near? It is a clear sky in which the endless heat is lost. It is a man of shadows. You! Who are you? Are you a man of shadows?

JUICY LUCY

It's the anchovy woman! Kill her! Kill her!

TRIUMPH

You demented half-crazed moron, shut up! I

beg your pardon, Miss Thing, you there! Have you had an accident? One of our House of Wax girls seems to have been under the sun too long and wishes to know if you might be the anchovy woman?

BENITO

I am Benito Bustello. Brother to Abolena Bustello. Companion to Fatima Velasquez. I play with the wind, talk to the clouds, and sing to the road.

DONNA BELLA BEADS

What do you do with the hatboxes?

BENITO

I will follow the eternal will that governs my destiny.

TRIUMPH

One so young to speak of destiny. Who has taught you of such things?

BENITO

My freedom is my inherent beauty.

DONNA BELLA BEADS

This one's on a trip. Let him drown!

JUICY LUCY

Let's face it, Big Bust, the police wear dresses because they like to wear dresses!

BENITO

I have a feeling that I'm going to be the most handsome man in the world.

WARNER

I just wanna be loved. No matter how bad I am.

MALA

If anyone mentions happiness, swim for shore!

MARY

I am an enemy of the American government.

DONNA BELLA BEADS

Come into my mouth, you fool.

BENITO

I don't care about you other bastards. I'm gonna be great and famous!

CAREER

Don't let these police humiliate you. They become more and more fantastic every year. They are turning you all into dirt-eating slaves. They represent a few stinking-rich people who don't even stay in this country most of the time while they march everyone else into huge anonymous housing projects and don't allow them to even take a dog home with them.

BIG BUST

He's ugly because I can't have him.

JUICY LUCY

I want to have all my emotions out on the
screen.

BENITO

I want to kiss the harps of angels.

ABOLENA

Make it not be true, make it not be true.

MADONNA

Have you tried God, my child?

ABOLENA

Benito, who's the weirdo?

MADONNA

Do not be frightened. Yay tho' I walk through
the valley of the shadow of death I will fear no evil
for thou art Walt Whitman.

MALA

Hey, spics! Knock it off.

BENITO

It is the superstition of all witches that the
shoes from a dead man's feet will bring years of
good luck.

TRIUMPH

Who are you, woman?

BENITO

She is Fatima Velasquez. Formerly billed as the veiled wanderer. She doesn't exactly do the dance of the seven veils, but she does do a pretty colorful number with an army blanket.

WARNER

I'd like to see that!

CANTA LUPE

Surely the woman is not mute.

BENITO

No . . . she is not. You should hear her talk.

TRIUMPH

I'd like that.

FATIMA

There is a pageant in the sky tonight. And nature wears the borrowed light of history.

WARNER

Let her keep the shoes. Those soldiers were dead anyway.

MALA

I'll bet they're nothing but Gypsies.

BIG BEAD

They're human.

CREAM VARLETT

They're SCARED.

WHEELS

It's the revolution.

DONNA BELLA BEADS

The past is past. I suggest we forget it and wait for dawn.

FATIMA

Skip the talk. You won't regret it.

TRIUMPH

Have dreams and schemes sufficed to keep man alive. His hands, his back, his honest sweat are the natural tools by which man can survive.

FATIMA

They keep private their bitter tears. Cannot you too mourn silently?

CANTA LUPE

A silent man is dangerous.

MALA

His calm cloaks secrets he must keep.

TRIUMPH

Night that shelters all creation in shadow and silence has failed to still her. I heard you say it. Yes, indeed, she's a lulu.

BENITO

You're the one who requested she speak.

TRIUMPH

Yes, I was. Wasn't I?

ABOLENA

The vision of the future was so clear, so sweet she jumped for joy, Benito. She jumped. She really did, she jumped.

TRIUMPH

All men dream joys few men can attain. I dream of my castle in Spain. Like fools, like friends, like you. I feel the warm sweetness of waking dreams and their soft appeal. Their truthless flattery lifts up my weary soul. All wealth is mine.

Fair women kneel. I challenge foreign tyrants, I will have their heads. Oh, I'm wise. Oh, I'm loved. I am king. I'm bright and kind and brave and free, until Career Kit calls and then I remember the plain self I was born to be.

CAMINADA

Noccalula white buffalo zamilu el toro tortuga Imparato Osopo Cusimano . . .

CANTA LUPE

I suppose you and your kind think when you take some poor devil of a girl, starving for a little comfort and happiness, and make of her a thing that good women won't look at.

I suppose you think your measly money pays

the price. Pays for the homes you ruin, the mothers' hearts you break, the girls you send to hell! You pay! No, it's the woman that pays ... and pays ... and pays!

                    WARNER
                  (To Big Bead)
           What's with Canta Lupe?

                    BIG BEAD
         She's talking to the Spanish Army again.

                    WARNER
Oh.

                    CAMINADA
It's a mirage, you know.

                    WARNER
You're a mirage too. You gotta be a mirage. I just don't believe you're here. Any of you.

                    CAMINADA
Give him some quinine water.

                    TRIUMPH
I suggest we try to rest.

                    WARNER
Suggest something else.

                    TRIUMPH
Rest is best.

WARNER
(Takes out a stiletto)
No, really, suggest something else.

MALA
Good government. The game great heroes play. Demanding the death of Vanity.

WARNER
Solitude, where I have known joy in my youth that I still cherish. Shall I never come and bar the loud world from the shadowed freshness that you are?

MARY
Who would hinder me, alone among your dim aisles? To the nine sisters that instruct me in the skies. Were my verses to paint them, it would be enough. Faith chose no golden threads to weave through my life. They are deep, as deep as prodigal, as deep as pleasure.

MALA
I vow fate new tribute. Pressed from ocean leisure.

MALA, MARY, AND WARNER
When the moment comes and death I have met, I'll have lived without cares—to die without regret.

TRIUMPH
(Grabs her and points heavenward)

Behold our limits, the sky! I will lend you my
wings.

FATIMA

Lend me your money. I don't want your wings.

TRIUMPH

What's this? You cut me to the quick!

FATIMA

How long will you abuse our patience? None
dare oppose you. The Great Triumph Avenue and
his Pig Alley! Well, I'm of a restless breed. I feel like
I gotta travel on.

TRIUMPH

And dream, if fenced in, of just how far you
might go. Mad with hot dreams of lasting fame.

FATIMA

You lie! Though fools are courted with lies, I
am not.

TRIUMPH

I have never lied about Donna Bella Beads. She
stuffed herself with self-congratulations. Age spoiled
her looks. Farewell, love and adulation. One empty
year passed. Then two, worsening her plight. Regret
set in. Older with each day, she felt this charm, that
smile, those tricks, even LOVE, grew pale, till her features shocked and displeased. Then came the paints,
the dyes, the creams. Hundreds ... but none eased
her losing fight with time, the impalpable thief.

FATIMA

But desire can have its way, even with the proud.

TRIUMPH

We prize the beautiful. The useful we disdain. Beware: the moment of greatest danger arises when the battle is won.

FATIMA

Run! Since men kill men! But who cares who is my master? No enemy army irks me. I just hate the man who works me. Frankly, war is YOUR disaster.

TRIUMPH

An owner has the surest glance.

FATIMA

I'd like to add lover's glances to that list.

TRIUMPH

The moon was full.

CAMINADA

We and the cosmos are one. The cosmos is a vast living body, of which we are still parts. The sun is a great heart whose tremors run through our smallest veins. The moon is a great, gleaming nerve center from which we quiver forever. Who knows the power that Saturn has over Venus? But it is a vital power, rippling through us all the time.

CHRISTIAN FAITH

All of this is literally true, as men knew in the great past, and as they will know again.

BENITO

Underneath all the tales there does lie something further, something different. How different? The thing which is invoked is of a different nature. However, it may put on a different appearance or indulge in its servant's human appetites. It is cold, it is hungry, it is violent, and illusory.

Craig Highberger

Vain Victory was a huge hit even though the reviews were wildly mixed. The *New York Times* reviewer called it "unabashed trash . . . the quintessence of Camp." Al Goldstein's *Screw* gave it a rave, singling out Paul Serrato's song "Who Are You?," originally written for *Lucky Wonderful*, a duet performed by Jackie and Candy Darling, and also the breathtaking, stage-splintering ballet performed by Ekathrina Sobechanskaya, "the world's most beautiful 6′6″ hairy-chested ballerina." The *Village Voice* review panned *Vain Victory*, calling it "awful, abominable, execrable, beyond description and beyond belief," but Paul Serrato recalled that Jackie loved the impassioned criticism because it only helped fill seats. Curtis's ads for the show contained a notable quote from one of the celebrity attendees: "The best play I've ever seen"—John Lennon.

Paul Ambrose

On *Vain Victory*'s opening night at La Mama, I was backstage putting on my makeup, and Ellen Stewart leans in and says, "Now, honey, don't be nervous, and don't be scared. But there may be a *bomb* in the room. So if you've got anything illegal, the police are coming." And my lipstick went right across my face. And, within moments, everybody is running in and going through their things to take out all their drugs and hide them. And the next thing I see is the police going through the folds of Madame Sobechanskaya's tutus looking for bombs—she was a six-foot-six-inch-tall ballerina, and the tutus were huge. This postponed the opening by hours. It turned out that Ondine hadn't been able to cop in time, so he called a bomb threat to the theater, knowing it would delay the play.

Jackie had advertised *Vain Victory* in the *Village Voice* with a list of practically everybody who was anybody in New York, and Jackie was powerful enough and liked well enough by everybody that everybody she had advertised was in the show showed up. They may have just stood there in the background of a scene, or did like Andy Warhol as the winged avenger: all he did was stand up and take photographs during the play every so often. It was really a who's who of the underground at the time. I remember peeking into the lobby at one point and being tickled pink because not only was the lobby packed with people, and the street outside, but Marion Javits, who was the wife of then Senator Jacob Javits, was standing there, with a big party, screaming, "I'm Marion Javits. What do you mean I can't get in?" We were that sold out.

The opening of the show was like a twenty-minute rant by Ondine to a pair of legs on a couch. All you see is the legs and feet and Ondine, screaming, "Look at those feet, look at those god-damn feet! Those feet once tread the high wire. Now look at those filthy feet. You're going to go back where you once started—washing out elephants' assholes!" The language—I just couldn't believe it, but the audiences ate it up.

The show was an enormous hit; we ran sold out for weeks and weeks. But you know we never actually got to the end of act three, and nobody ever missed it. The first act took place in a circus. It was originally going to be a ship, the SS *Vain Victory*. The second act was an underwater ballet, which lasted about five minutes. Clarice Rivers, the artist Larry Rivers's wife, was the lead chorus girl in that scene. The third act took place in Lana Turner's bedroom in *Peyton Place*.

Candy Darling was the leading lady, and Dorrian Gray was the nearest thing to a leading man we had, except for Ondine, who came and went depending upon the drugs. He was brilliant when he was there, but one night he came in and walked onstage after Douglas Fisher had been doing his part for some time. Douglas was afraid to tell him he had been fired, so they both performed the part in tandem. Jackie let it happen, but the rest of us were terrified, because Ondine was dangerous. He never attacked Jackie. Like two scorpions, they were wary of each other.

Styles Caldwell

One night, Paul Ambrose and I were walking home from a gay dance somewhere in the Village, and Paul was wearing a black leotard with pearls and a fur hat, and Jackie Curtis came up to us and said, "I'm doing a play at La Mama called *Vain Victory*, do you want to be in it?" And, before I knew it, we were both over there at La Mama, rehearsing.

Originally, Jackie was going to play the female lead, but he changed his mind and decided to play the male lead, Blue Denim, and he had Candy Darling play the female lead, Donna Bella Beads. Each act of *Vain Victory* was several hours long—the complete script was never performed. . . . It's a wild script.

A 1950s high school graduation opens the show, and Mario Montez came out in a fabulous gown as the valedictorian and made a speech. At one point, there were two guys in leather jackets simulating jerking off with their backs to the audience. And there was this actual shell of an old car on stage that represented the James Dean death car, and Jackie perched in it and sang one of his musical numbers. . . . Then the play transitions into this story line about Candy Darling, who plays a mermaid. She and Mama Mermaid were in a lagoon over in one corner of the stage. They amputated Paul Ambrose's legs and gave them to Candy, so she could become this glamorous movie star. Paul spent the rest of the play rolling around in a wheelchair. He played a character called Marie Nemo. He came to just hate that name, because for many years, whenever people saw Paul on the street, they would scream, "Oh, *Marie!*," whether he was in drag or not. It got on his nerves because even strangers did it—people he didn't know who had been in the audience. Marie Nemo was some Italian woman; during rehearsals, we were walking around one night, and Jackie saw this building in Little Italy, the Marie Nemo Building, and he made that the name of Paul's character. He was good at coming up with fabulous names. Jackie was brilliant at putting shows together. Before we opened, he found this shop with all these incredible old costumes that went back to the Ziegfeld Follies, and for a hundred dollars, we got about two dozen gorgeous outfits, including the mermaid costume.

In the show, Stephen Holt played a character called Nunca the Divine. He was brought out on a litter and sang a song, "I Am Nunca the Divine"; I think *nunca* means "never" in Spanish, so he's singing "I am *never* the Divine." He played a lot of parts, including Mama Mermaid in the lagoon, and Jackie had him wear a white wig and sunglasses, made up so he looked like Andy Warhol. It was kind of a tribute to Warhol. The character was a stage mother like Mama Rose in *Gypsy,* screaming things at Candy like, "Go on, honey, push your way in there, honey, get right in the spotlight, you can be a big star!"

One of the characters I played in *Vain Victory* was a cigarette girl like they used to have in nightclubs; you see them in some of the old movies from the forties. I came out in drag carrying this box hanging around my neck, filled with absurd things. I walked right across the stage, interrupting the play, and walked right out into the audience, screaming, "Cigars, cigarettes, rubber dollies, French letters, hair burgers!," just bringing the show to a halt and offering all these insane things for sale. It drove Paul Ambrose crazy because this was during his most dramatic scene, but the audience just loved it.

We were packed every single performance; this was the big downtown hit in the summer of 1971. Every night was wonderful and unique. . . . One night, Silva Thin, one of the performers, tossed a lighted cigarette and it landed on Stephen Holt's litter, which had all these ribbons and colored paper fringe, and during the play it suddenly caught on fire. Of course, everybody screamed and carried on, and all the actors and the audience ran out into the lobby and the street until a couple of stagehands dragged it outside and put it out with a fire extinguisher. It was like it was part of the show.

Jeremiah Newton

Candy Darling and Jackie were just wonderful on stage together in *Vain Victory*, and Candy liked Jackie a lot. But Candy did not approve of Jackie's excessive alcohol and drug use. She told me she thought Jackie was out of control. That kind of behavior upset her. Candy liked a feeling of security. She liked knowing where she was going to sleep at night. She couldn't stay with Jackie because she was afraid her things would be stolen or her dresses ripped up.

Unlike Jackie and Holly, Candy always behaved in a very grand manner. In 1972, after she appeared in Werner Schroeter's film *The Death of Maria Malibran*, Holly and Jackie made merciless fun of her serious attitude. It just drove them crazy that Candy aspired to be a working actress and a legitimate movie star. "Get real! Get off your trapeze and down into the sawdust!" Jackie would tell her.

Jack Mitchell

I photographed Jackie as a man with Candy Darling when he was doing *Vain Victory*. Candy looked very much like Glenn Close at that time. Candy was the opposite of Jackie, because she was very serious about her femininity, her makeup, her glamour, and her clothes. Unfortunately, Candy had very big feet. But Candy's Jacqueline Kennedy/Marilyn Monroe voice took the illusion right over the top. Candy could go anywhere and no one would question it. Holly Woodlawn had the zaniest sense of humor of all of the three ladies. She seemed to me to be a kind of sexed-up ZaSu Pitts on drugs. I am so pleased that Holly, as the only surviving member of that trio, is in Hollywood living her own legend.

Paul Serrato

Joe Franklin was a very famous TV personality here in New York City, and a very good friend of Jackie's. He had a program called *Down Memory Lane*, and nostalgia was his stock in trade. Jackie of course loved old movies, old movie stars, and old music, contemporary though he was. This is one of the crazy contradictions about Jackie, but it also makes him very interesting. Joe Franklin decided to have Jackie and Candy on his show the summer that *Vain Victory* was such a hot thing downtown.

Jackie and Candy went on the program, and Joe introduced them as the new romantic couple from the downtown theater scene. Joe, God bless him, did not know that Candy Darling was not a woman. When he found out afterward, after the program, he was very upset with Jackie, and I think it might have ended the relationship. But it was very difficult to think of Candy as a man.

Joe Franklin

Nobody discovers anyone, but I gave the first exposure on TV to Barbra Streisand, Al Pacino, Bette Midler, Dustin Hoffman, Eddie Murphy, Bruce Springsteen—the list is endless. Among those that got their first exposure on my show was Jackie Curtis. When I think back on some of my all-time highlights, I remember one particular show with Jackie and Candy Darling. They were doing a show downtown called *Vain Victory*. And they were so lovey-dovey on the show; I thought that Candy was a lady, because she was so beautiful, and I really thought they were boyfriend and girlfriend.

You've got to believe me, out of a half a million interviews—I'm in the *Guinness Book of World Records* with the longest-running talk show, twenty-eight thousand episodes of the *Joe Franklin Show*—I look back at that one with Jackie and Candy and scratch my head and say it really couldn't have been—but it was!

Holly Woodlawn

I was in *Vain Victory* for part of the run in 1971. Nobody ever knew what the story was about because everyone was so bombed and high. Miss Candy Darling was a mermaid named Donna Bella Beads, and every night the play changed because nobody ever remembered their lines. So finally Miss Darling quit the show. She said, "I refuse to work with nonprofessionals." So Jackie had me take over her role, and the next night Miss Darling came with a rich society boyfriend and sat right in the front row, because she wanted to see what a disaster I would be playing her role, Donna Bella Beads. Backstage, we were crockola, honey. The vodka and the speed were rampant.

So here I was in Candy's mermaid costume in a wheelchair, and it was my first time making the entrance, and I started rolling the wheelchair and I didn't know how to make it stop! So the wheelchair rolled right over the footlights and the little front wheels went off the stage! I fell screaming right into the front row of the audience and landed literally in Miss Darling's lap—and she leapt up, pushing me off of her. She was screaming blue murder, accusing me of doing it deliberately! This absolutely brought the house down. Both the cast and the audience were completely hysterical. Here I was, stuck in this mermaid outfit, with my legs strapped together, and I was seriously drunk, and I could not get up, so everybody picked me up and reseated me in the wheelchair on stage, while Miss Darling and her date just stormed out of there, cursing and ranting. The audience loved it and applauded. They thought it was part of the show. People came the next night and were disappointed I didn't catapult into the audience.

Agosto Machado

At the very end of the run, pretty much the entire in crowd had seen the show. The big celebrities came very early in the run. Here it was just a week before closing, and Dotson Rader brought Tennessee Williams to see *Vain Victory*. So all during the show, we were all sneaking peeks out into the audience to look at Tennessee. I guess he was a little parched, because he took out a pocket flask of something and was sipping at it every now and then during the first act. Slowly, during the second act, I noticed his eyes close. I thought, Oh, he's listening to the text, listening. But then he slouched down in his seat with his head slumped to one side. I thought maybe his neck is sore so he's resting it. But he was there in the audience! For the entire show. Okay, maybe he was asleep during the second half, but he did wake up at the curtain call and applauded. Tennessee Williams applauded *Vain Victory*. And we all came down and thanked him for coming, and he was so kind and generous with his praise, and chatted with Jackie and Candy and all of us.

Then, later, Tennessee Williams was so generous, helping Candy Darling by casting her in *Small Craft Warnings*, which debuted at the Truck and Warehouse Theater, across the street from La Mama. During that run, Tennessee had to fill in for an actor that had to drop out of the show, and he had difficulty memorizing his part, so he had to have script pages all over the set, on the furniture and the bar. And sometimes he got mixed up or missed a cue. It was downtown theater. It didn't matter if he got lost. It didn't matter if he demanded a real drink from the bar. You keep the play going. It's what we all did in Jackie's plays. You work around it. There were times Tennessee sat down and there would be an incredibly long pause while he had a drink, and someone from the cast would bring him a script page, and he'd take it and brush them away, saying, "I know, I KNOW! I wrote it!" And by the end of the performance, he was inebriated, but it was Tennessee Williams! It was downtown New York theater, and it was art.

Paul Ambrose

During *Vain Victory*, Jackie was doing so much speed that he got quite thin, and he became absolutely demented. He believed that the spirit of Gary Cooper had possessed him, or he had taken over whatever powers Gary Cooper had, and Gary Cooper's daughter, who was a friend of Jackie's, did not discourage him from believing this.

Joey Preston

My mother, Josephine, worked in a lot of [Jackie's] shows. They would always argue about her getting paid. My mother wanted to get paid for her work. She played the part of the librarian in *Vain Victory*. Every day, she'd take the bus down to the theater and perform and come back home very late. She worked in a spaghetti dress. She did a striptease and sang a song. But she wanted to get paid. They used to fight about that all the time, but they loved each other tremendously.

Agosto Machado

Vain Victory closed the night that the Cockettes opened and bombed at the Anderson Theater down the block. Only Jackie and I did the full run of performances. Jackie had this magic carpet, and I was going to hang on for all it's worth, because I thought after Jackie Curtis, after this fabulous acid trip of *Americka Cleopatra* and *Vain Victory*, I never wanted it to end. It launched me into the downtown art and theater world.

Young people today, when I lecture, will ask, "What was the budget for the sets and costumes?" I say, "What budget?" We went out on the street, and to the thrift shops and the Salvation Army if we had big bucks, and we just found what we needed. It was nonprofit theater. To the young people today who immediately ask, "What do I get paid?," I say, This is an experience; you're going to work with people who are part of the history, and why is the money so important? I know today it's a different world. They just cannot understand how we could actually put on a show without money. But Jackie did—you saw the essence of make-believe, the muted reality of fantasy and possibilities.

CHAPTER 7

Cabaret, James Dean, and Poetry

For Craig And Andy
from Jackie and Hud
Christmas '75

Jackie in Hollywood photographed in James Dean mode just before auditioning for the role he felt destined to play. (Craig Highberger Collection)

There Is an Aura About Them
A poem by Jackie Curtis

From across the room, even without my glasses.
There is an AURA about them.
It's funny too, because they're wearing
just any old clothes.
But they will choose their colors.
On your left there is Stanley Perring.
On your right, Jackie Curtis.
There is an AURA about them.
Who are they?
No matter how much is indicated on the wall
directly behind them
there is still that aura.
There always WAS that aura.
They are smoking, True . . .
and the dog is fighting with the cat.
Stephen Arbex is asleep in the back room.
There is a parachute on their ceiling
and a shrine near a window that reads
or rather announces GIRL MACHINE
flanked by photos of the Virgin Mary,
Candy Darling and Lana Turner.
In an authentic church relic
that might very well be real gold
and once held those religiously kept flames,
there is encased a tube of lipstick that Carroll Baker
gave to Jackie Curtis.
There are dead flashbulbs on the window ledge.

They rest in peace.
Three Penguins and a copy of Back to Godhead.
Half a dressing gown adorns the center window.
There is a champagne bottle (empty) on the third windowsill,
which has growing on it more than an artificial flower,
it is quite justifiably the number 8.
The number of new life.
There is so much in this one room
(and there are other rooms with just as much, or little)
that one feels transported to some other time,
or other place . . . but never really quite forgetting
exactly where you are.
Each of these people, truly are, people . . .
or are they? truly?
They are devoured by all
and all is devoured by them.
It is simply quite awesome.
One must stand back,
unless there are those who prefer to take
the proverbial giant step and become closer.
Anything and everything seems to be possible . . .
if you dare.
But keep your eyes open,
unless it is a kiss you want . . .
there is an aura about them.

Paul Ambrose

Jackie started his nightclub act at a club called Reno Sweeney's, and eventually he and Holly Woodlawn did one together called "Cabaret in the Sky" at the old Huntington Hartford building, the New York Cultural Center, at Columbus Circle. Curtis openings were really special; everyone pulled themselves together and dressed to the nines for them. I remember silent movie star Hope Hampton showing up with an entourage—you've never seen more pink wrinkled flesh and diamonds in your life; she was the blondest thing I had ever seen.

Holly Woodlawn

My favorite time working with Curtis was "Cabaret in the Sky: An Evening with Holly Woodlawn and Jackie Curtis" at the New York Cultural Center at Columbus Circle. Everyone thought that Jackie and I hated each other, so we developed this funny introduction. Jackie would perform her set first.... [then] she would sing the first few bars of "Stairway to the Stars," then she would suddenly stop in midphrase and slam her hand angrily down on the top of the Steinway grand, yelling, "Stop the music! Stop the music!" There was stunned silence in the audience, and then Jackie would say, "You know, I really don't mind being the warm-up act for that Latin from Manhattan, Holly Woodlawn, but you should know we've got her locked upstairs in a cold rubber room . . ." The audience just loved it. Of course we didn't hate each other. Curtis and I were sisters; we were girlfriends—cut from the same cloth. "Cabaret in the Sky" was a tremendous success, and we wound up every show by singing a duet of "Just in Time" with our arms around each other. It was the most amazing and wonderful time, the most pleasure I have ever had performing with anyone.

Andrew Amic-Angelo

I will never forget the summer night in 1974 I was in the audience for Jackie's performance of "Cabaret in the Sky." That particular night, for some reason, there was a large group of leather men in the audience. Maybe it was some motorcycle club. There were at least four or five tables of maybe twenty men, all in leather, seated right up front. They had the whole regalia, leather chaps, pants, vests, and leather jackets with chains, leather caps, and boots. And this was unusual. And after Jackie performed one number, "I Enjoy Being a Girl," there wasn't much reaction from these leather guys . . . and Jackie walked downstage and right up to one of the tables and said, "You guys are so quiet. What are you, an oil painting?" And then he turned and headed offstage, saying, "Looks to me like there's a lot of Old Masters out there tonight." The entire audience was on the floor. And that was entirely spontaneous, witty, and apropos. It gives you an idea of what a brilliant performer and artist Jackie Curtis was.

Michael Musto

In 1968, Jackie lived as a woman twenty-four hours a day; she sort of became Marisa Berenson. But then she got tired of it. In 1972, she returned to facial hair; she/he returned to being a man. And, in 1985, Jackie looked back on that era, and told me this: "I'd say I'm tired of being Jackie Curtis, and somebody would say, But you have to be. We need Jackie. But it was a chore. And I was already turning my autosuggestive possession into a reincarnation of James Dean. I wanted to play James Dean, so I became him."

Jackie

People told me I looked like James Dean, even when I was in drag. And, strangely enough, there, on my birthday in 1973, there was this theater in the Village showing his films. And I got to see all of them, and I realized how much I looked like him. And I went home and looked in the mirror and started becoming James Dean. I thought they wanted me to do that. I thought that's what they want—you know, the gods from the great beyond. I thought they were tapping me on the shoulder and saying, "If you do this for the rest of your life, you'll be in, you'll be untouchable, you'll be invisible—you can do whatever you want. We know that you're great, but if you can do this then you can marry the princess, and have the king's gold, and ride the white horse into the sunset."

Taylor Mead

Jackie Curtis and Candy Darling both tried to be Kim Novak, or Lana Turner. And then, of course, as in the Lou Reed song, Jackie became James Dean for a day, but actually Jackie was James Dean for nearly a year. And then, without any announcement or anything, shifted gears again.

Harvey Fierstein

Jackie's life was very much the performance. Jackie wanted to be a star—that ambition was very real. Jackie's way had never been done before. And especially when Jackie went into male drag and did the James Dean thing, I thought, What the fuck is she up to now?

A letter from Jackie Curtis to Mona Robson:

Jackie Curtis
7606 & One Half Fountain Ave.
West Hollywood, CA 90046
October 7, 1975

Dearest Mona:
It is Tuesday night and it is about 20 after 10 by now. Well this looks like the final stretch. They have begun the casting for JAMES DEAN: PORTRAIT OF A FRIEND. Here's something about how it's going. William Bast (Jimmy's friend and roommate

*of about six years) is the writer director & co-producer. He writes
the teleplay and a production company JOZAK down at BUR-
BANK STUDIOS is hired to handle the production end of everything. William Bast waits for NBC TV to give a firm picture
commitment so that he can retain most of the control over the
project. NBC TV finally agrees that William Bast has control. All
during this long debate over what will finally go on the screen, an
actor from New York City makes his way out to Hollywood. His
name is JACKIE CURTIS. He arrives June first because they tell
him casting will begin at the end of June. No such luck. But meanwhile Jackie lands a job on RHODA which of course enables him
to join Screen Actors Guild which we know will help Jackie in the
long run with James Dean. Or James Dean is helping Jackie to
prepare for the long run, or SOMEBODY is helping Jackie besides
Jackie! Thank you somebody! All you some bodies!*

    *Next story (same theme): Barbara Malarek arrives. She is a
writer. She is also well acquainted with Jackie Curtis having
talked with him when she and David Dalton were getting the
James Dean THE MUTANT KING book together so she knows
why Jackie has come to Hollywood. Barbara has already sent Bill
Bast a telegram and a photo of Jackie signaling his arrival. So
aside from this one "In" and this first initial mail to Bill Bast,
Jackie has been loyally playing the game by submitting his picture and resume, proof sheets and color photographs of himself
every other week as time passed while he was laying low in Hollywood. And time passed. And as time passed Barbara arrives.
We learn of the firm picture commitment from NBC before THE
HOLLYWOOD REPORTER or anybody because Barbara can
call him up because she was at Bill's house with David Dalton to
interview him for the book too. Bill Bast tells Barbara, "We have
to see Jackie Curtis because I am SO aware of Jackie because
everywhere I go friends and people I know keep saying, 'Have
you seen Jackie Curtis yet?' or 'Have you met Jackie Curtis yet?'*

so there's no question about seeing this young man." But still when I call the production company they say, "The casting is now out of our hands and we suggest you get yourself an agent to submit you to the casting director because an agent will make you seem more important and that's the only way the casting director will see you, Jackie." So now I am involved in a frantic search for an agent or a manager.

I just joined the Beverly Hills Health Club to maintain my movie star physique along with Charlton Heston and Burt Reynolds. I am in MOTION PICTURE MAGAZINE this month, Janet Charleton's INFO MANIA GOSSIP COLUMN, and tomorrow when the VILLAGE VOICE comes out (Wednesday) you will all read about me in BLAIR SABOL'S OUTSIDE FASHION column. What more do they want? Yes I know. They told me. An agent. I'd call Sue Mengers but she's handling some important business matters with Andy concerning the new movie BAD. So already I have a new movie looming large in my future.

I just finished writing George Cukor about my predicament and asked him whom I should see since I met him a few years ago over dinner. I am racking my brains over this! Please Mona help me keep this thing alive! I want you to alert all the keepers of the flame, anyone who is involved in silent prayer and who has been keeping the faith. I am not about to let this thing die. I will not kiss the prospect of landing this role good-bye before I can kiss it hello and breathe into it some sort of real life's blood. Help us back from the grave. *I am serious.*

Otherwise the weather is gorgeous and REBEL WITHOUT A CAUSE will be showing a week after WR MYSTERIES OF THE ORGANISM out here. I love you and miss you very much and hear you are now a redhead! I hope you are being a good girl and taking special care of your sanity. Give all my love to New York. Now PRAY and remember THOUGHTS ARE THINGS.

I love you Mona, JACKIE

Styles Caldwell

When Jackie came out to Hollywood, he started taking male hormones and working out at the Beverly Hills Health Club. I remember he went around in a sailor outfit he bought at an army-navy store, and he looked very masculine and sexy. He was away from New York City for the first time and he felt really free, like he was starting over completely. Jackie and I moved into this apartment down on Fairfax with this guy who went by the nickname DDT, those were his initials. DDT's mother was an M-G-M contract dancer and his father was a cameraman, and Jackie thought that was fabulous, and said, "DDT, you are a true child of Hollywood." We both fell in love with him. Jackie was greedy, he wanted him to himself, but Jackie liked a lot of different men. Here was an entirely new city to explore, and Jackie ran around a lot, and he was very annoyed that I moved in on DDT. He'd come in and find the two of us fast asleep in the same bed, and you could just tell it made him jealous.

Jackie sought out Vampira; she had some kind of shop in West Hollywood where she sold stuff. Vampira had been a friend of James Dean's, and Jackie wanted to hear everything about him. Jackie also became friends with Jo Van Fleet, who had played James Dean's whore mother in *East of Eden*. But things didn't work out. Jackie went to the audition and didn't get the part, and it really broke his heart. He believed in miracles and magic and reincarnation and he really believed he was destined to play James Dean, and it didn't happen, and I felt very, very bad for him.

We were invited to this big party at the home of a famous movie producer from the 1930s. Andy Warhol was the guest of honor. Everyone was there, Verushka, Pat Ast, Jack Nicholson, everybody. Jackie worshiped Andy, but Andy was not very friendly that night. He didn't act surprised or happy to see Jackie. But Jackie met a casting agent at the party, and she got him a part on the sitcom *Rhoda*. Jackie had this great scene with Julie Kavner, who played Brenda, and Valerie Harper and Nancy Walker. The episode was "Brenda Gets a Roommate." He played this odd character that was obviously a man in drag. I was in the studio audience for the taping and it was hilarious. Valerie Harper gave him an eight-by-ten of herself that she signed "It was wonderful working with you, Valerie Harper" that he was very proud of. But they cut his part completely out of the episode, and nobody bothered to call and tell him. Jackie was terribly embarrassed because he had told all his friends and relatives, and even called Andy Warhol and told him when to tune in. Shortly after that humiliation, Jackie gave up on Hollywood and moved back to New York City.

Note from Jackie to Paul Serrato, undated (spring 1977):

Dear Paul,

Here I am, it's somewhere between 2 and 2:30 P.M. Wednesday. For some reason I was absolutely positive our rehearsal was this afternoon. Now that I am sitting here and find that you are not in, I am faced with the horrible fact that I made a boo-boo. Or else you are out walking Gretel. In the event of my making a boo-boo I guess it's because Monday and Tuesday things just seemed to be happening non-stop and without checking I raced up here with the same pace as the last two days. Now I realize our appointment must have been Thursday at 2 P.M. and I could have rested today. For myself it isn't so bad but I asked my guitar player to meet me here and only gave him your phone number because I am forever forgetting "325" as in 325 W. 22 St. I am really a dope! Anyway while I sit here God knows what he may be thinking.

Oh well, in a little while it will be all rectified and of course I shall see you tomorrow as we had planned. In a way I will use this experience as a drill. My mind is so focused on this gig I will let nothing come before it. It is an important engagement and my first New York City public performance in a good while. When I say everyone will be there (some will come both nights) I am certain it will lead to something more. This is it. My emergence; my rebirth; et cetera. All sorts of people will be in attendance to witness it and they will be seriously appraising the entire performance.

In keeping with this spirited and positively fierce determination I wound myself up too tight and like a clock that is fast I came 24 hours before the appointed time . . . all right. I'm just going to have to keep better track of these weekdays because I hate making such unnecessary mistakes. Anyway the owner of the club told me it would be all right if I used a drummer in the act—what do you think? Do you know a fabulous drummer who would work with us? It would really jazz up the act and also add that pulsation that sends the audience into a wave of hysteria when a performance is gyrating to the primitive rhythms, as it were. Call me later or I'll call you. I figure if you were walking Gretel you would have been back by now. I'm certain our appointment was for tomorrow, so I'll speak to you later and we'll work tomorrow.

Things couldn't be progressing better! I can't wait to begin rehearsing (that's an understatement I suppose). The room (Lady Astor's) is so beautiful, our space is just great—the owner is tops and the deal is tremendous. It's very exciting. Already everyone is dying to see what it is I can possibly be up to—me too!

XXX With a song in my heart for you: JACKIE

Excerpt from a handwritten letter from Jackie Curtis to Steven Hall, written while he lived in Elisbethton, Tennessee, with his father, stepmother, and half brother, Tim Holder, for several months, dated June 24, 1977:

Dear Steven,

Yes, New York City can be hateful. I suppose Hollywood can be just as intense. Maybe that's why they are both such fascinating cities. I do prefer LA to NYC. I've always enjoyed working in New York City, and not working in NYC—but I can't stress how much more alive I've felt while working. Recently before leaving NY I recall a few private conversations with some very close friends and I remember saying something like "I will never get used to this darkness." So many times while sitting idle in NYC I began to doubt whether I was actually alive. About doubting my sanity, well—that is another thing. I guess being sanitary is being sane enough, you know? Have you ever heard of the insanitation department? That's what they once called those of us who went to school on the streets.

Tennessee is light; airy; cool; warm; not at all hateful and as many of its inhabitants refer to it—"God's Country." I began driver's ed classes last week and will finish by July 8th. That's when I will start searching for desirable employment. It took me long, lonely, but oh so valuable hours to decide to split . . . but once the thought patterns change for the better, they must have their cycles perused. I was going to type this for you, then it would have been longer . . . a bit more prolific, but as it happens my brother is asleep since he's worked from 11 P.M. to 7 A.M. and the electric IBM would awaken him, to be sure. There are a few other things I would like to explain to you about my departure from NYC but at the moment please believe me the words have escaped me.

Your new friend, Jackie

Excerpt from a typewritten letter from Jackie to Steven Hall, dated September 2, 1977:

Dearest Steven,

I had to come to LA; my father suggested it because my step-mother was getting resentful of all the time my Dad and I were spending together. After all those years I go back to re-acquaint myself with my Dad and my step-mother doesn't really dig it, at all, so my Dad says to me, "Maybe you'd be better off in Hollywood." GREAT SUGGESTION, DAD! So here I am at the fabulous Gracewood Court . . .

XXXXXX Jackie

Holly Woodlawn

I was doing my nightclub act at Reno Sweeney's in 1977, and Jackie came with some friends. When I came on, she shouted, "Gay gown!," and heckled me and was a real bitch. One night after the show, Curtis invited me over to watch *Mildred Pierce* on the *Late Show*. And when Butterfly McQueen came on, Jackie said, "I know her. I know Butterfly. She's very sweet. We talk on the telephone all the time." Of course, I didn't believe a word she said. And then Jackie was doing her cabaret act at Slugger Ann's a year or so later, and there in the audience was Butterfly McQueen—it was true! She was friends with Butterfly! How odd is that? The truth is truly stranger than fiction.

Craig Highberger

At NYU, there was a class in directing for the stage. One scheduled exercise was to have several different students direct the same content, simply for comparison's sake. The selected scene was from *I Am a Camera*, John van Druten's theatrical adaptation of Christopher Isherwood's *The Berlin Stories*. I persuaded Jackie to come in drag to the class and play Sally Bowles, the role Julie Harris played in the 1955 film. Jackie was perfect as the Depression-era Berlin party girl. She wore her Greta Garbo gray wig, and a little black dress with scarves and carefully selected jewelry. Jackie was astonishing in the scene, and the professor acknowledged that Jackie was much better than any of the "real" girls who played the part.

Steven Watson

I met Jackie indirectly through a network that involved the "Hot Peaches," which was a very important gay gender-fuck kind of cabaret musical group in the 1970s. Their first show was at Jackie's place on Second Avenue. Through the Hot Peaches, I came into contact with Minette, who I think of as the great drag godmother of them all. And Minette loved Jackie. Minette sent Jackie a Christmas card, which he had pinned up, and it was signed, "Jackie, you're a corker—Minette." So I decided I wanted to interview Jackie and went to his room above Slugger Ann's, and I walked in and Jackie was cooking a huge pot of spaghetti, and he dumped it out into the colander and steam kind of filled the room, and it felt so Jackie in that it's dramatic, and it's about cheap food and bulk—a very Jackie moment.

Part of what fascinated me as I interviewed Jackie is that there was this incredible kind of emotional ping-pong that was both brilliant and kind of scary, because it was driven by so much need. It was very tangible, that in your contact with Jackie there was something he wanted from you—which was attention. It was around the time that Jackie's mother died, the late '70s. And Jackie would call and insist that I meet and interview him. And I remember during one of the interviews Jackie had the movie *Rebel Without a Cause* playing on television without any sound. We could both see the screen, and Jackie would periodically stop the interview and give some of the James Dean lines, which was quite eerie.

I saw Jackie in the James Dean boy phase and in the girl drag phase. I saw Jackie's so-called return to drag at Slugger Ann's, and Jackie came out wearing Slugger Ann's wedding dress, and Jackie was both glamorous and bossy and totally dominant and confident. The whole thing was a wonderful kind of dramatic badge of courage. Then I saw Jackie perform as a boy when we did the book *Minette: Recollections of a Part-Time Lady*, and that night Jackie appeared as a boy wearing just a simple white shirt, and he sang the song "A Quiet Thing" and it was incredibly vulnerable, it was a whole other side that Jackie allowed people to see.

Tom Weigel

It was Andy Warhol who first introduced us. This was at the Coe Kerr Gallery in New York on December 2, 1977. It was a reception for the opening of athletes, silk screens of sports legends. In strode this tall figure with a pixielike face. "Jackie, you're wearing summer clothes," was the first thing Andy said, then, "Tom, this is Jackie Curtis, and, Jackie, this is Tom Weigel, he's a poet." Jackie just grabbed my wrist and forearm like I was immediate property. I could feel a spirited current pass between us, something incredible and final, like a New Testament event. We were friends from that moment on.

Andy asked Jackie what he had been up to. Jackie said he had just gotten in from California, where he had been for some months, doing screen tests for *The James Dean Story*. I just couldn't see such a giant figure as Jackie struck actually taking on the part of James Dean. After all, Jackie himself was infinitely more interesting, and anything but distant.

I was going to the St. Mark's poetry readings by night, and school at Parsons, and then over to Slugger Ann's to visit Jackie. Jackie sometimes tended bar there for his grandmother Ann, who was very possessive of him. She had brought him up while his parents were separated. Jackie's mother had died shortly after we had met. I was new to the family, all Italians on his mother's side. Jackie called me his producer right off the bat and brought out his two S & H scrapbooks. He wanted to make a comeback. I was stunned. This person had done too much already, and he wasn't even thirty.

Jackie had nonstop gift for words and creative speech, the like of which I shall never encounter again. And his quietness was just as profound. He was so real, so up front, as they used to say then, that he made other famous persons seem like pointlessly stuffy nonentities.

I moved into the Lower East Side early in 1978, to 515 East Sixth Street, a third-floor studio. My place became a publicity office for Jackie. His comeback was well under way, and we planned it methodically. My building had a charming Curtis Company elevator, just the right touch for all the future cast parties I would hold there for him. I started up a small-press magazine for poetry and select prose called *Tangerine,* and printed scenes from his plays and prose poems he was writing then. Jackie was then writing *Champagne,* and something entitled *Moral Heights,* a sort of alternative soap opera. He was on the *Joe Franklin Show* from time to time, and working very hard.

His poverty shocked me, so I had to help out with ready cash, and helped get him on welfare, just so he could subsist. I claimed we were roommates and splitting the cost of my apartment. I provided letters of update when periodically requested. Jackie had a building and mailbox key, and was on good terms with the kindly super at 515, Mrs. Savitch. He picked up his checks this way, and sometimes a gift box from so-and-so, like when Barbra Streisand sent him an entire collection of her record albums. He would give us crash courses in Broadway musicals and old Hollywood movies that came to us free on the *Late Show*.

Michael Andre

In 1979, we were preparing the *Poets' Encyclopedia* for publication, and we sent out different invitations to poets, and "B-Girls" arrived—that's Jackie's poem. It's really the best fit of all the works in the encyclopedia. Poetically, it's a tremendous success. It blends the kind of epigrammatic qualities of Alexander Pope, and uses a lot of alliteration, which nobody else uses in the *Poet's Encyclopedia*. It's like a medieval poem; it's just b, b, b, b, and then he gets into a totally whimsical, drunken-rant kind of work, and I could tell immediately, from the first ten lines, that it was a wonderful poem.

I immediately thought that he'd created, like Eliot's *Waste Land*, some large structure and then chopped out the underpinnings, the different movements—which makes it sound like the drunken ravings of a B-girl. Dramatically, it moves toward the classic climax in a B-girl's life, which is getting . . . how should we say it? . . . making love in a bar. It was such a compendium of perfect detail that I didn't know where he got it, and when someone told me he lived over his grandmother's bar, Slugger Ann's, I knew that he had been observing this kind of behavior all of his life. And identified with it, and understood it in a kind of disinterested way. And lived it. Unfortunately, I guess. After he wrote this, he began to live this life.

The poem also particularly reminded me of the poetry of Gregory Corso, who had the ability to take a single word, a concept—marriage is his most famous—and explore the whole meaning of it. "B-Girls" is sort of a distorted mirror image of marriage. Gregory was a junkie, all his life, which was a very long life. Unlike Jackie's, unfortunately.

The reason I think there was originally a structure to the poem, that he removed, is because the movements have different forms. He will use a lot of jokes with rhyme: the bar girl . . . someone wants the bar girl's cherry, but the bar girl has been around the block so many times that she's afraid of only losing her olive. Then he'll get into very fancy and colloquial alliterations using the best everyday language . . . that, as written, is very meaningful—but also, as written, sounds like a drunken slut.

Throughout the poem, alcohol is the water that keeps the whole desert alive. I guess it's why it keeps reminding me of the *Waste Land*, because it's a lot about dryness, but instead of having Hindu philosophy save the day, nothing saves the day. Or sex in a bar after-hours saves the day. In fact, it sort of ends with obliteration. It's a poem with a lot of color, but not much hope.

B-Girls
A poem by Jackie Curtis

> G-girls are by no means to be confused with B-girls!
> But what could make so vast a difference between such
> lonely initials?
> The Hollywood Horizon stretched out in front of us
> offers a simple palm tree to start with.
> So it is with the B-girl.
> One highball to get her in a movie star mood.
> And then she is identified at once by the loneliest
> initials ever strung together on one string of
> B-girl beads. . . .
>
> The B-girl is or WAS a basic type of barroom boarder
> bordering on boozey bursts of the cash register

to remind her
in her bleached-out bourbon bender
it is time to beg the boys for a brand
new batch of 100 proof hootch to heave down the hatch.

The blisters of her backless mules begin to bring
the B-girl to an alcoholic so-existing coherency.
Bothering these brawny bachelors with blatant wedding bands
to buy her one more Bloody Mary.
The beating of her bongo brains breathes
Benzedrine into bathroom walls
where the B-girl can decipher her fate.
A frenzy sewer fumes
and faulty toilet fixtures
where strains of a nickel's drop into the jukebox bucket
only brings Miss B a bleary eye.
And an earful of what was once a royal flush is only now
a quarter to three
and no one's in the place except for Miss B.
Very B, this Girl.
Not a BAD sort
just a bouncing
maraschino cherry of a ballbuster
mesmerized by that sleazy swizzle stick.
The B-girl's calling card is a cognac-drenched coaster
that spells out for her what no first-grade textbook ever could
ALL GONE GIRL.

The B-girl is an endless commodity of
comic strip
straphanging
horseplaying
pushpins
from one end of the bar to the other.

The Bs have cold knees
they snort
they sniff
they even sneeze.

Friendless frails in flapping fringe
found long lost near a beer barrel
cramped
like creatures who kick
to keep moving.
Watered down
their spirits pass,
chit and chat
an eye
of someone.
YES it's him.
The handsome stranger
swooning over "B."
His kind of woman.
His kind of promise
to continue
could result in risking
cash sales
for water and World War One whiskey
by order of the management.
The B-girl does a round
with not one word in her defense
lapping up the liquids
reeling from the fracas.

Other B-girls squint and totter
what's the matter?
Someone's got her.

So, the swinging doors fly creak-free
the clattering clack of class-lacking heels
parading poorly past the pieman
on her way to where?
Searching the air for fiery fumes
of fabled Fleischmann's feathering her drunken nest
slitted skirt insures a spring and a swing
to her gait
after all men
that IS the thing.
Down the beer-stained trodden hall of hate
B-girls from her impure past forget to wave
and fly fast.
Her sweat-streaked bar stool
that stung her calves and thighs to sleep
have found another lazy Susan
plucked and plastered
like a willow planted firm she'll weep.
The men
make time
the clock has told of ticking trips to tense amour
kindred spirits shut the door.
Love is strange
the poets say
but B-girls rhyme from day to day
striped halters draped on dames
in dreams of Drambuie
draining the billfolds of the buckskin badmen
breaking the B-girl's arm
before asking for her cherry.

So many makeshift hearts of
rock and rye

precede a reply of
"Only an olive"
obliterating firing facts of
realities rifles
when the B-girl announces that her
cherry has been chewed
out by champion cheapskates
who drag her through barroom after barroom
and setting no bail.
Like a semiprecious prisoner
Her last mile consists of not an electric chair
but a park bench
plenty available for the B-girl's bottom line.
The same bottom line signed
so many spritzers of lime ago.
More yellow than green by now
Miss B begins to wander
washed-up
from saloon to supermarket.
Our B-girl's dream of walking down an aisle come true
only in an A & P
with a shopping cart by her shabby side.
Side by Side.
And she ain't got a barrel of money
but even a B-girl's gotta eat
and so brilliantly versed in the art of deception
our chowsy frau plays tricks on suspecting eyes
proving to checkout counters once again
that the B-girl can at times be thought of
as no better than a common thief.
Especially when apprehended, as our heroine was
is and always will be.
The eternal spiritual virgin

at the last minute
and at the missing mercy of some man
haunting her heart's
only normally employed regions.

Pumping her in, pumping her out,
this gorilla's bride, so to speak.
Like a stranded jazz singer
searching for the proverb
searching for the proverbial lost chord
so prone to the suddenly and responsive striking.
Only the cactus casts shadows that cool the sand
which is still and stretches far out into an effortless
night nature mature
and a habitual repeat performance
employing the desert's vast supply of the four winds
if only she could make a wish
make a wish
to abandon the four winds for Four Roses
so quietly invisible to her naked B-girl's roving eye.
On and off again, water faucet fumbling at the tap
that B-girls look to like farmers look
to the red harvest moon
for promises of fulfilling fertile earth's promise
to sprint up a bounty of multiplying tables
so serenely set
and ripe for reaping hands
whose seeds have been sown.
Horns and blind men
wheels of a fast, fast car.
Occasional streamers of headlight.
Underneath it all
there she lies

trapped like a fox in the South
during a most precipitous festivity.
But still her threadbare throat
remains parched as the dunes in a daring desert
movie blaze beneath blowing torrents
of too much hurricane
and only occasional musical comedy
mirages
of the M-G-M Lion and Mickey Mouse
reenacting an Aesop's fable.

And as if all life were not one gold-plated hell of a
cheap charm bracelet to begin with
the B-girl is faced with the Motel alleyways
that lie to her weaknesses.
Sentimental arms spread heavenward ever grasping
that hallowed homemade jam and jelly.
Our B-girl is being followed.
It is 4:15 A.M. Accompanied by a navy blue
blanket up above.
Warm and woozy
she travels twisted toward the soda pop machine
chewing her Technicolor red lips
wishing for a miracle
could this attention from behind
merit her attention span
which is geared to a bottle filled with bubbles?
Any bubbles will do.
In her human condition those voices tell her
to humiliate herself further
and be grateful to God for a sign.
No it is not neon.

She is being paged
by hand
grabbed by the rump.
It was all coming back to her.
That area the strange grasp was exploring
was once married to marshmallow soft cushioney security
in strictly dishonorable surroundings.
Slurping sleeping powders in cheese-flavored champagne
from Tunisia.
But a B-girl travels in trespasser's footsteps
so no doubt the incident occurring between the hungry hand
and the unsuspecting pair of victims (her buns)
secondary characters in a charming situation
where actually on her way to the soda pop machine
in a desert motel setting
where her course was diverted by steel trap fingers
frantically feeling
and grabbing at life.
Ah yes, she was still alive, she mustn't forget.
In silent concession their private procession begins
at the closing door.
She's open
receiving
fast love they're achieving.
Both wining like greedy gamblers
carousel like rooms
existing upon driftwood porches
attached by pink picket fences
and dead, dim silhouettes
of sordid sunset scenes
slapping the world
outside the waiting window

who wants to win.
The B-girl is no fool
she knows she must deposit the correct amount of change
if indeed any
so with the confidence of an Arista member
she makes to her sexual accoster for the fare
for this ride that the fizzy fake pop will take her careening on.
Drunk enough to bring dangerous destiny
within his waiting foyer where his laymen's loins once appeared
loyal and alive, now grinding with a scissor sharpener's fervor.
Sparks begin to fly
as far as where Miss B has been biting clouds
of very close chummy dust.
Having been in more accommodating situations with lovers
she sloughs it off
but in point of fact is totally aware of what this
lurid tongue
was traveling to find land in her jungle of rain.
Yes, her jungles were storming the gates
the tigers ever burning bright
drizzling then flooding
mere mortals monsoon
and on the paper plate of an end table
was blaring a secondhand plastic portable radio
what was that song again?
Oh yeah
she remembers.
C'est magnifique.
And it was.

Lily Tomlin

Jackie was a natural satirist, because he was an outsider and an artist. All the notions he had about living and being made him really able to see the absurdity of the culture. Plus, as Jane would say, they were sitting home all day taking drugs and watching TV. There's no quicker way of seeing the absurdity of the culture!

I remember one reviewer said that Jackie Curtis played female characters without pretending to be a woman. Jackie was an artist—whatever he wants to express, it's just organic, it comes from inside of him and he puts it on outside—it's him sort of shaping the world and creating his own sort of world order, like Bush's new world order, and, I must say, Jackie's was a little more tantalizing!

Leee Black Childers

Jackie couldn't stop observing humanity, and writing. Holly Wood-lawn is a great comedienne. Candy Darling was an incredible beauty, a magical beauty. But, of the three of them—and it's always going to be the three of them—Jackie was the brains. Jackie thought it all up. And sometimes, maliciously, she made it all up: "Oh, Holly, you look so beautiful in that shower curtain. Let's go out! That's such a good idea, we'll just pin it around you just like this and then we'll just run in the streets!" Jackie loved that kind of thing, and Holly would fall for it because she was the clown.

Joey Preston

Curtis was our nucleus; he was our star in the family. I worked with Curtis as a stage manager and business manager for most of his productions during the eighties, and I just loved working with him. But my curtain went up on time. Sometimes Curtis was half dressed, and I'd say, "Curtis, get dressed, the curtain is already up," and he's screaming, "What're you doing to me, what're you doing to me?"—as he's trying to get his hair up and his makeup on. But we had a very good working relationship, and I love him dearly.

Michael Musto

The first time I saw Jackie perform was in 1983 in a play called *I Died Yesterday*. She played screen legend Frances Farmer, who was lobotomized. That was a popular story at the time—Jessica Lange was playing the part in a movie; there was also a TV movie—but I really think Jackie's version was the best. She just came on stage in a wig and a dress, no accoutrements, no falsies. She was just Jackie as Frances Farmer. She played it really broadly. There was a lot of pathos inherent in the story, and I thought that she got to the pathos more than the Jessica Lange version, more than the TV movie version. She got to the true essence of Frances Farmer. And Ondine, another Warhol superstar, told Jackie: You're perfect for this part because you already look like you escaped!

Penny Arcade

I played a lot of ancillary roles in Jackie's plays, supporting roles. And by this time I had started to do Margo Howard-Howard, who is best described, at that time, as a fifty-five-year-old drag queen with the body of a woman and the head of a fish. Jackie and Margo were absolutely inseparable for quite a long period, from the late seventies through the eighties. Margo was a junkie and a madman who had convinced New York that he was a she, because nobody would try to look like that in drag. She looked like a seventy-year-old dowager in drag, and had convinced New York society that she was the niece of the Duke of Norfolk. It was a phenomenon, unbelievable, and Margo was the president of the Mary Stuart Society, and Jackie's personal drama coach. At any rate, to amuse everyone, and myself, I would always imitate Margo.

During the run of I Died Yesterday, Jackie fired the actress who played the hairdresser role and came to me and asked me to pick up the role. So the first night I did it sort of as myself, and I found it kind of boring. So the next night I was walking to the theater and I found a pair of plastic-framed glasses on a garbage can on East Third Street with no lenses in them, put them on crooked, as Margo would, always disheveled. And that night, without telling anybody, I played the hairdresser as Margo, and Margo, of course, was there in the audience every night. I knew I was on to something, because all the actors in the show gathered in the wings and were watching this nondescript little five-minute scene of Jackie playing Frances Farmer getting her hair done by a lunatic studio hairdresser, and I started chasing Jackie around the stage with a coat hanger, saying, "You don't need a hairdresser; you need an abortion! Your hair doesn't need a brush; your hair needs a coat wire! Your hair shouldn't be brushed; your hair should be tossed!" It was MAD, absolutely insane, and everyone went wild.

CHAPTER 8

Champagne, Drugs, and Death

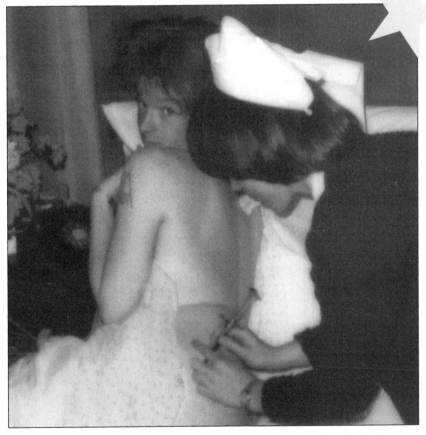

Jackie in St. Vincent's Hospital receiving an injection in 1974 after losing a kidney due to a mugging. Ten years later, he would be admitted after overdosing on heroin—less than a year before his death. (Photo by Craig Highberger)

The Dead Are Dancing with the Dead
A poem by Jackie Curtis

The soul is the desperate hope of a man
that he may live forever.
A hope and a delusion.
Doesn't the soul live on after the body?
The soul does not exist.
The pyramids in Egypt harbor skin and bones
which would be more useful to the earth's fertility.
But man yearns to be immortal,
even to the extent of preserving his dust.
Is immortality so cherishable?
The desire for immortality is in the nature of things.

A stone thrown into the air yearns to fly on forever
and struggles against the wind that hinders its speed
against the earth which pulls it back to its bosom.
Once the wheel turns it must complete its dizzying career to the
*   end of time . . .*

The voice breaks into echoes
that it may not vanish and become
part of the silent air . . .

Petals of a flower battle
against the cold hands of winter.

Nothing willingly relinquishes its form and condition.
Man is like

the stone and the wheel
and the flower
and the voice.
His ingenuity and fear, however,
have created a shadow
which lives on forever . . .
His soul.

Robert Heide

My favorite memory image of Jackie is a visit to Candy Darling's deathbed. Myself and John Gilman and a crazed actor named Tom Ellis, who worked with Tallulah Bankhead, were there. There were roses, and Candy was propped up in bed. Then in comes Holly Woodlawn and Jackie, covered with glitter. And the TV goes on, and they're sitting on either side of Candy, watching the soap opera *Peyton Place*. And Tom Ellis makes the comment: "This is the real *Three Sisters*." Somebody should have staged a version of Chekhov's *Three Sisters* starring Jackie, Candy, and Holly. Can you imagine what a sensation that would have been?

Jeremiah Newton

In 1974, when Candy Darling was dying of cancer in the hospital, Geraldine Smith, Tinkerbelle, and I were there with her constantly. We were Candy's support system. Candy was in that private hospital room like a queen. Candy had all of these photographs of herself pinned up everywhere. Lots of people would send her flowers; instead of throwing them out when they died, Candy insisted we keep them all there. It was an amazing sight, all of these rows of vases filled with wilted roses and bouquets, with the live ones in the foreground. It was like a memorial display of death in life.

Jackie and Holly came to visit one afternoon. Jackie, Candy, and Holly were just hilarious together. They would play off of one another. I remember Candy saying, "You know, Holly used to work for the American Kennel Club. She's a real dog, that one." I remember Holly and Jackie sat there and ate an entire box of Candy's chocolates, and most of her lunch tray. They tried to get the nurse to bring them lunches too, like it was room service. Lauren Hutton had come to visit sometime earlier and brought Candy a beautiful makeup bag completely filled with very expensive Ultima makeup. After Holly and Jackie left, we found that some of it was missing. So they were banned from coming back into her room. Candy was furious and very hurt.

Jackie

I want to be a serious actor. I want some dignity in my life. The drag life just drove me to the edge of my sanity. I was a superstar, along with Viva, Edie, Bridget, Jane Forth, Candy, Ultra Violet, Joe, and Taylor, but that's all over now. There is no underground. Half of them are dead now. I saw a fellow in drag at a party last night. He had long painted fingernails. He wanted to be Holly, Divine, Candy. He made me feel depressed. It's degrading in the eyes of God. It's a violation of yourself, your family, and your God. I did it. Candy did it. It's done. I spent three weeks in the hospital when I had a kidney removed in 1974. Candy Darling had just died. It gave me time to think. I knew I held the rest of my life in my hands. You only have one trip. I want to be a movie star. I want a legitimate occupation. I want to work, not fool around.

Harvey Fierstein

Most artists, unfortunately, really believe that the craziness is part of the art. I have friends that will die drinking and drugging. Although I think it's killing their art, they think it's part of their art. You don't have to be a tragic figure. I think Jackie was always destined to be a tragic figure. Her way was not my way. She did drugs; I did alcohol. Much better to do alcohol, because it's so much more accepted.

Gretchen Berg

When Jackie was in his early thirties, he was really addicted to some kind of drugs. He told me that he had gone to St. Vincent's Hospital once in the middle of the night. He felt he was having a nervous breakdown, crying, and saying, "Please help me, I can't control myself anymore, I can't stop." Once when he came over to visit me he was so high he was falling down, unable to walk. I had to hold him up. He was talking a mile a minute about things that didn't seem to be very important. The drugs and alcohol were taking over.

The last time I saw Jackie was a few years before his death. I ran into him on Fourteenth Street. He was dressed as a man. His hair was very short, and he was nervously chain-smoking. He was no longer the Jackie I had known.

Jackie

Last week, I walked past a manhole cover and steam was coming out, and I realized that Manhattan really is Brigadoon. It actually is. And now I worry constantly about crossing the line, because I know the spell will be broken forever and I will never be able to return again. I had a special meeting with my psychiatrist and my alcohol counselor to tell them I'm not panicking.

Laura de Coppet

I have never known anybody as attached to drugs as Curtis was, and particularly amphetamine. He felt that without it he was worthless, or that he couldn't create. I kept telling him, No, no, Jackie, that's not true! But nothing could convince him otherwise. And, somehow, I understand that. But it was tragic. Because he was sui generis. They broke the mold after they made Curtis. He was a genius. A hilarious one. I counted him among my best friends, although I did know that, like all drug addicts, the drug [came] first.

Robert Heide

Jackie was into pain. I'm not saying Jackie was a masochist, though I'm sure that was there. But there is the story Jackie told about not just going for electrolysis but going to someone who pulled the hairs of Jackie's beard out one by one, and how very much it hurt. While Jackie was telling us this story, he was smiling. Suffering for one's art, or one's persona. Becoming the image of the star. God knows, Jackie was a star, in the firmament of not just Andy Warhol but off-off-Broadway, and Christopher Street, and wherever Jackie turned up.

Jackie was not averse to slumming in gay bars or waterfront holes or truck stops or diners; I think that's the kind of *Vain Victory* aspect of Jackie's life. The last time I saw Jackie was at Boots and Saddles, a bar on Christopher Street. Jackie was James Dean that night. And Jackie was also incoherent that night. There was a little bit of glitter on [his] face.

Sasha McCaffrey

When Jackie Curtis was doing a show, she lived in another world until the show closed. Her nightlife never ended. Doing the show was nothing. On the stage, Jackie was on autopilot, but the maintenance, awaiting that hour on the stage—that was what was difficult. That took a lot of effort. I was one of the people Jackie wanted around her all the time when she was doing a show. When I'm do-

ing a show, I don't want anyone around me. You can't see me before the show. We had totally different ways of approaching our
craft. Jackie needed an entourage close to her at all times during
the run of a show. So the first night she did *I Died Yesterday*, the
Frances Farmer story, I went home with her, and was with her constantly until the end of the run. The other bosom buddy during
the show was this other drag dream, Margo Howard-Howard, who
was her spiritual adviser and drama coach. So it was the three of
us, the three gay musketeers, jamming into a cab every night, going to the theater, partying, then coming home together. Sometimes Margo and Jackie would be talking to each other and I
would feel totally invisible, like I was watching a scene from a Lana
Turner movie. It was flawless.

But there were little things behind the scenes I didn't notice at
first, like the fact that Margo was shooting loads of heroin. One night
during our revels, Margo had gone to the bathroom, and Jackie and I
heard this chilling scream. The next thing we know the bathroom
door bursts open and Margo comes running across the room at full
speed in her underwear. And BAM! She slams into the living-room
wall, like she didn't even see it, and she just drops to the floor like a
stone. Jackie and I looked at each other in total shock.

I went over to Margo. She was unconscious and completely mo-
tionless. I touched her face and stomach and was horrified because
she was clammy and cold. It looked like she wasn't breathing. I
screamed, "Oh my God! Jackie, she's dead!" And Jackie just dismis-
sively says, "Oh, Sasha, Margo is not dead." And I screamed, "But,
Jackie, she stopped breathing! She doesn't have a heartbeat! We have
to call an ambulance right now!" So Jackie hurries out of the room to
call 911. All this time, Margo is still not moving or breathing at all.

In a minute or two, I hear a commotion in the kitchen, and
Jackie comes running back in. She hasn't been on the telephone.
She hasn't called 911. Jackie has changed out of her stage costume
and is now wearing a fucking nurse's uniform, complete with the

little white nurse's hat and a different shade of lipstick. And in her hand she has one of those big two-pronged kitchen forks, the kind that you use to hold a roast when you're carving it. And as I watch, Nurse Jackie gets down on her knees and just jabs this great big fork right into Margo's ass—stabs her with it, like she's just a side of beef. Sure enough, Margo sucks in a huge breath, starts breathing again, and screams out in pain. Jackie throws the fork across the room, saying, "See, Sasha? I told you the bitch isn't dead!" Then Jackie just calmly sits down on the couch and lights up a cigarette. And there is semiconscious Margo, scrabbling around on the floor like a half-dead cockroach, bleeding from a fork wound. I thought, You know, this is incredible. I've never witnessed behavior like this in all my life, and I probably never will again.

That was just one night, just one average night. And Jackie's play had a two-week run. Two weeks of this madness. You think I'm leaving after that? I'm not going anywhere. Two weeks in drag, two weeks of not sleeping, two weeks of perpetual partying. It beats anything. Is it living theater? Is it living art? Maybe. Whatever it is, even if it's just foolishness, it sure beats war.

Eddie Snyder

I first saw Jackie at Max's Kansas City, which was a hangout for the Warhol superstars. I was one of the guys at the bar drinking beer. I didn't know Jackie Curtis was a guy then; I thought she was some really hot babe. I thought she was too good for me.

In 1981, I had lost my job, and at night I was sleeping in a sleeping bag in the Westbeth Theater. I was friends with the owner, and he would lock me in there at night. I met Jackie, and he told me I could move in with him. He was living in Slugger Ann's old apartment on Twelfth Street. She had died, and Jackie was taking care of his uncle Jackie, who was schizophrenic and on disability from the Veterans Administration. So both Jackie and I became his caretakers. But Uncle Jackie began to get worse and worse, to the point where even with medication he became unmanageable. Aunt Josie came over and saw that the situation was really impossible, and Uncle Jackie ended up in the VA Hospital. So this burden was lifted from us. But it was a difficult time. Jackie was trying to get a project together, but nothing was happening. And so the two of us were watching soap operas during the day, and Jackie was drinking too much. And this was no good. So he went to detox a couple of times. And he went to Cabrini Medical Center and got a good alcoholism counselor, and started going to twelve-step meetings, and really got himself free of dependency. And his friends rallied around him and helped.

While preparing his play *Champagne* for production in late 1984, Jackie started doing heroin. At one time, that was my drug of choice, and, believe me, once you start doing heroin it's not easy to resist. Jackie overdosed, and one of the people she was with, Margo Howard-Howard, did not correctly inject the antidote into a vein. The shots went into the muscle, and both of Jackie's arms developed abscesses. She was in St. Vincent's Hospital for about a month, which nearly derailed the production. But it went on.

After the play closed, Jackie stopped taking heroin. He realized he needed to transcend his Warhol superstar image, and he decided to concentrate on male roles. So he developed a new identity—Shannon Montgomery—and began to live it. He was really gung ho about it. At this time, I had moved out to my own place. And a week before Jackie died, I visited him, and you would not have recognized the apartment. He had completely cleaned it out and had organized the place for the first time. Jackie was transforming into this new person, Shannon, and the apartment was changing too, because he was starting a new life. He never looked better. He had a great attitude. He was excited about the future and ready to work, and told me he was going to see his drama teacher's agent about representation.

But, unfortunately, he had friends that were using cocaine and heroin. And he had this drug dealer named Gomadi who adored him, and so she was coming over every day and supplying him with the drugs and taking them with him.

Jackie

Within just a couple of years, my mother died, my grandmother died, my uncle Tony died, and I had to send Uncle Jackie to a state institution. It was just too much for me, so there was nothing else to do but put on the dress and the glamour and the mink and go to the curb and scream "Taxi!" and go to work.

Joey Preston

After our grandmother died, Curtis lived in her apartment with my uncle Jackie for a while, before my uncle Jackie had to be put in a mental institution. And Curtis was complaining about Uncle Jackie all the time. "Get rid of him, he's driving me crazy, he's leaving cigarette butts under the mattress, starting fires, he'll burn the place down." After Uncle Jackie died, Curtis was letting a lot of people into the building at all different hours of the night. The neighbors started complaining, so the landlord started getting down on him. The landlord somehow got into the apartment to see what the place looked like. Well, it was a disaster. He saw an American flag from outside hanging in the window.

Curtis had all his posters all over the place. Nobody had ever complained. It was tasteful, but in Curtis's taste. [The landlord] calls my mother, who was in charge of my grandmother's estate at the time. So my mother goes out and buys a can of paint to paint the kitchen. She picked pink, her favorite color. I come in and I see Curtis sitting at the kitchen table, smoking. And there is my mother, who had just been diagnosed with cancer, who was very sick with five slipped discs and degenerative arthritis, up on a ladder, painting around Curtis's posters because he won't let her take the posters down. I was furious at Curtis. We often had these family fights. It happened a lot, but we still loved one another.

Penny Arcade

I spent a year with Jackie, almost every night, helping Jackie not to drink. Hanging out, talking, Jackie trying not to drink, and finally Jackie kicked the booze. Drinking was an enormous, enormous addiction for Jackie. Sugar. Booze. Heroin. Fame. Jackie's big addictions.

I went to visit Jackie just before the rehearsals had started for *Champagne*. And Jackie had an enormous bruise on the arm, where he had Andy's name tattooed. It was quite hideous-looking. Jackie told me that it was from being mugged, and I thought, This is kind of an odd injury from being mugged. It was all swollen and red. And then a few days later I got a phone call from Jackie and he was in St. Vincent's Hospital. He wanted me to bring him a vanilla shake and three packs of Kools—that was when you could still smoke in a hospital. It turned out it was an enormous infected abscess. It was loosely bandaged, and they had done some preliminary surgery on it, but it was like looking into the Grand Canyon, you were looking at bone, you were looking at muscle—it was grotesque. I was horrified, and yet Jackie maintained his story. Of course, he knew that I was completely dead set against him using drugs or alcohol, because of what it did to him. What had happened, I later learned from Margo, is that Jackie had OD'd, and Margo had given Jackie a salt shot, which is used to revive a person. And it had abscessed. And I said to Jackie, You can't keep doing this.

About this time, I started distancing myself from Jackie. I sort of have a sixth sense [when] someone is going to die. This has happened to me a number of times, that before a person dies I distance myself from them. About six weeks before he died, I ran into Jackie on the street for what turned out to be the last time. And he was very excited. He said, "Penny, I've changed my name to Shannon Montgomery." He was launching a male version of himself as an actor. He was dead serious about it. But it was all make-believe. It wasn't like, I'm going to be Jackie Curtis boy now. It had to have a new name because it was a new identity—it was an act. Jackie was involved in a constant state of make-believe. He told me he thought there was a big future for himself. He said he was auditioning for soap operas. But he had this otherworldly appearance. And somehow I knew that I was never going to see Jackie again.

Don Herron

In the early eighties, I used to stay up very late because they had two *Mary Tyler Moore* shows on, one at 2:30 A.M. and one at 3 A.M. I loved that show, so I would always stay up and watch it before bed. One night, the phone rang during the show. It was Jackie, and he said, "Don, I don't know what to do, I've been thrown out, my aunt threw me out, I'm out on the street, help me, please help me!" Well, I couldn't just hang up on him, so I said come on over.

He arrived and made quite a commotion because he had five suitcases, and one of my friends came out of his apartment to see what was going on and wound up helping carry things in. Jackie was a good bit overweight and sweating, and it was clear he was not ready for bed and I was, so my friend Adam said why don't you come spend the night with me and let Jackie have your place. So that's what we did. I said Jackie you can stay here tonight, and I will be back about nine o'clock. I sort of don't expect to see you, but that's when I will be back.

So at nine the next morning, I knocked on the door and there was no answer, so I opened the door and I saw, spread out on the floor in a long line, everything from Jackie's suitcases. He had unpacked everything and folded and organized things. It looked like an art display. Clothing was arranged. Shoes were arranged. It was as if he expected to sell the stuff. He wasn't to be found, but the bathroom door was closed and I heard a splash. So I went to the door and knocked and said, "Jackie?," but there was no answer so I opened the door.

Jackie had taken one of my old sheets and had torn it in half and drawn all over it in black grease pencil. He had hung it from the shower curtain rod, like a movie star swag. He had drawn over all the bathroom tile, the walls, and the ceiling with this black grease pencil. He had filled the bathtub with dishwashing liquid, and the bubbles had spilled out all over the floor. He had taken the grease pencil and drawn black dots all over his face, like he must have started with one beauty mark and gotten carried away. He was kind of huddled there amid the suds. My eyes were wide with shock, taking all this in, and I looked at him and said, incredulously, "Jackie?," and he replied, "I got a little crazy last night, but I'm okay now."

Mona Robson

Nineteen eighty-four was really a rough year for Jackie, and for me. We did a lot of crying together. I told him, We've spent half our adulthood high, and now we're crashing. We're just not going to be as happy as we were. So Jackie quit drinking and became the hospitality person at AA meetings in the Village. And, in 1985, he decided to take on this new identity, Shannon Montgomery, because he wanted to be just an ordinary actor and make his living that way. So Jackie changed his look completely. He cut his hair and let it go back to its natural color, and he had new photos taken as Shannon Montgomery and typed up a new resume for auditions. He also signed up for acting classes at the Herbert Berghof Studio in Greenwich Village, [which] was founded by the fabulous stage actress Uta Hagen and her husband. Jackie, or I should say Shannon, insisted that I enroll too. But he did not want anyone to know who he was, that he had been Jackie Curtis.

HB Studio was really wonderful because everyone on the faculty made a living at whatever they were teaching, like Charles Nelson Reilly taught comedy directing and Sandy Dennis taught stage and screen acting (we had to avoid her because Jackie knew her and did not want anyone to know that he was Shannon).

In class, he performed a scene with a young actress, from the play *The Owl and the Pussycat*, just beautifully. At the end of the scene, the first thing that our instructor, Bill, said was, "You know, Shannon, if you had been playing that part when the show was running on Broadway it would still be running today!" And that was so great because Jackie needed to hear that he was good, that he could be making a living at this. It was just the boost his confidence needed. The incredible thing is that this acting coach, Bill at HB Studio, had seen Jackie perform in drag in *Glamour, Glory, and Gold*. He just had no clue that Shannon was Jackie. That thrilled Jackie because it was what he wanted, to just slip into this new identity, Shannon Montgomery, and start over completely, leaving the past behind.

Penny Arcade

When Jackie was casting his final play, *Champagne*, at La Mama, there was a role that I wanted desperately. So I wrote Jackie a letter because I just couldn't bring myself to call him and ask. I wrote that I wanted this role, and I wanted to play it as Margo. And Jackie refused me, and that was very hard for me to take, because I promoted Jackie like nobody's business. So I just pulled back from the relationship and did my own thing.

I did my first solo performance at an underground club on Eighth Street in April of 1985. And opening night I was waiting behind the curtain to go on, and all of a sudden there is this big commotion minutes before the curtain goes up and here is Curtis with completely bleached-out hair. He has with him an enormous pile of flyers and a photographer to take pictures, and Jackie starts to perform a love scene, trying to kiss me. Now, back in the late sixties, Jackie and I would go out cruising all night, and at dawn would come home empty-handed and sleep together in the same bed, but we couldn't do anything because I was not a boy. It took me a long time to come to terms with that. So here is Curtis trying to make out with me, and I thought, What on earth is going on? It's like wish fulfillment.

Jackie gave me a bunch of his flyers and suggested that I throw them into the audience as the opening of my show, and I said, "Jackie, I have an opening." And I think this was an unusual situation for Jackie, because I had always been a supporting player in his shows, and now here I was doing my own work, which came out of Jackie not allowing me to have the role I wanted in *Champagne*. And what was happening was I had crossed a barrier that Jackie could not. Jackie had performed at the Pyramid Club in the East Village a few times, but his genius did not translate to that venue. Jackie's genius only translated to a handful of the gay boys who were going to those clubs in the early eighties.

So Jackie went into the audience, and every once in a while during the performance he yelled out to me things like, "Penny is my favorite coin in my collection," and "Penny is the illegitimate daughter of Jackie Curtis and James Dean," and I was looking at Jackie—with that brassy yellow hair, the enormous eyes, this otherworldly appearance—and I had a bellyful of heartbreak for Jackie. On a visceral level, I knew that Jackie had to lose.

Ruby Lynn Reyner

Jackie cast me in a male role in his last show, *Champagne*. I played the boyfriend, and before we opened he fired me. I walked in on

Jackie in the dressing room before a rehearsal and found him shooting heroin. I said, "Listen, Jackie, I can't be around this, you are going to kill yourself." I blew up at him because, just one month earlier, Eddie Snyder and I had taken him to the emergency room because his arms had abscesses from shooting up. Jackie hated hospitals and doctors and didn't want to go, but we forced him, and it was a good thing because his one arm was so badly infected they didn't know if they could save it. He almost had to have his arm amputated! And here he was shooting up again. I was just furious with him and said, "I am not going to watch you kill yourself!" And he said, "Okay, then you're fired!"

CHAMPAGNE
A comedy by
JACKIE CURTIS

Scene excerpt.

DEWIT
Gemaine Lefevre, the big bringdown. She'll bring you down once, twice, and, given the chance, three times. Someday she'll be put away where she won't be able to bring anyone down ever again.

GERMAINE
Well, I hope it's real soon! I'm eager for those padded cells!

DOM
You were eager for padded shoulders in the forties. See how selfish you are?

ASHES

I'd like to be a big Broadway star in a play just like this.

DOM

You have to eat a hundred jars of cold cream, eighty-seven tissues as well, and then you have to drink the urine of the hunchback from Equity. If you can pass that test, you must come up with enough money to join the swimming team at the Billy Rose Aquacade, write a short essay on "Why stardom means so much to me, and who the hell are you anyway?" Old fogies and chauffeurs will feel you up, tear your clothes right off your back, and humiliate you in front of six and a half usherettes who will be throwing lit kitchen matches at you furiously, while chanting an ancient primal growl and scream. But when you hear the audience loving and accepting the horseshit you present to them nightly, you'll know you're home free, champion of the flesh, and happy medium of the expression, and that's when you'll end up in the bins.

ASHES

When can I start?

Paul Ambrose

In 1985, on the opening night of *Champagne*, Jackie came out on stage with chiffon bows tied to each wrist, because she thought it was chic to show that she had abscesses and scarring so bad that both arms had to be operated on. They were covered in bandages for the opening of her show. I thought that even for Jackie this was not right. Too extreme. It just gave an indication of how much Jackie had changed.

Ruby Lynn Reyner

[Jackie] had supportive friends; he knew people wanted to help him quit, but he still chose the dope. It was such a waste of talent. I was very mad at him that he died like that. At the wake, I wanted to go up and slap him in his casket, but somebody restrained me. Some of the people there wanted to lynch Gomadi [his drug dealer] for her part in his death. I think it was a case of unrequited love. And when Jackie overdosed, Gomadi tried to have sex with him while he was unconscious. She just let him die. It's such an ugly end to an extraordinary life. But things worked out the way they were supposed to. A few months later, Gomadi gave herself an overdose and died. Or maybe somebody gave her a hot shot.

Joey Preston

The day Curtis died, I sat in the middle of the living room, right on top of the drug paraphernalia, I didn't move it, and I cried my heart out. I found Curtis's address book and I called everybody up. Everybody was upset and sobbing on the phone.

Penny Arcade

When I heard that Jackie had died, I wasn't surprised. I was working somewhere and checked my messages, and someone had called and said, Did you hear about Jackie? ... which was a horrible, horrible phone call. I called Jackie's aunt Josie, and ... by midnight, I was with the people who Jackie had been with. By midnight, I knew as much as I was going to know about the circumstances of Jackie's death, which were terrible, because Jackie didn't have to die. Jackie OD'd at 1 A.M., and people stayed in Jackie's house shooting drugs, coming and going all day, while Jackie lay there slowly dying. There was a woman there named Gomadi, she was a Kali worshiper, you know—she worshiped the Indian goddess of death. She was also a junkie, and totally obsessed with Curtis, and she had said to me, "Jackie and I were lovers," and I was, like, Are you insane? If anybody was going to be lovers with Jackie, it was I. Jackie was not bisexual; Jackie was hardly sexual.

Paul Ambrose

Jackie took a lot of speed. The good thing about speed is that Jackie was able to write play after play after play and then have the energy to actually do them, and only be insane part of the time. Onstage, it didn't necessarily appear as insanity, but just as the brilliance that it really was. But if you take a lot of speed, you don't get any sleep, and if you don't get any sleep you need something to take the edge off your nerves so you end up taking things you should not take. Heroin is one of the worst of them. Jackie started doing heroin. Somewhere in the back of his mind I think it was the "heroin chic" thing—everybody was doing it, Sid Vicious was doing it, John Belushi was doing it. All the really hip people were doing it, and it was there, and Jackie was never one to turn down a drug.

It did not help that he was hanging out with a creature called Gomadi. I was very wary of many people I was meeting with Jackie at the end, but Gomadi was weird. Weird with a touch of evil. Smarmy. She dressed like a Gypsy. I don't have anything against Gypsies, but if you are not a Gypsy you probably shouldn't dress like one. Gomadi was supplying heroin to Jackie, and, like many girls, she had a crush on Jackie.

Jackie was on heroin with Gomadi and overdosed. When you overdose, you get an involuntary and endless erection. And the story is that Gomadi started having oral sex with Jackie, and what

Gomadi thought were Jackie's cries of passion were the gurgles of his death rattle. Supposedly, she was so high on heroin that she did not know that Jackie had died. I like to think that that's the truth. There are others that think she let him die. The truth is, it was Jackie's first time having sex with a woman, and it killed him.

Harvey Fierstein

This horrible drug dealer girl brought some heroin to Jackie and shot up with him. And Jackie overdosed, and this girl thought that if she could suck on his dick and get him to have a hard-on or an orgasm that it would bring him back to life. So instead of calling 911 and saving that very special life, she did the bright thing that she did until the body was cold. If you put that in a play, would anyone ever believe it? If you put it in an underground film, they would say this is for prurient interests, nothing like this could ever really happen, no one could do such a thing.

Penny Arcade

So I said to Gomadi, "What are you telling me, that Jackie had his first heterosexual experience while dying?" And Gomadi said to me, "I gave Jackie shiatsu." I said, "For overdosing on heroin? Why didn't you call 911?" But even as I said those words, I knew that Jackie would not have called 911. People who live in the tenement slums don't call the police. If they die, you stuff their body behind a bathtub if it's a shooting gallery, or you drag their body outside, like Eric Emerson, who was hit by a bus. And Jackie had done the same thing the year before with Margo. It was just a miracle that Margo didn't die.

Michael Arian

Jackie's death happened at a time when many of us were doing a lot of drugs. Obviously, Jackie was at her zenith of drug use, or it probably would not have killed her. . . . Jackie was involved with a very fabulous group of drug users and dealers that were great artists in their own way, as was Jackie. And it just got the better of her. It was sad, it was very sad. And I was called in with others to help clean up the mess after she died. It was only to protect those of us who lived through it.

Tom Weigel

The overdose of heroin that killed him was truly accidental, happened because a sinister dealer from Washington was in town with a suitcase of uncut stuff. Jackie was not a junkie, and had beaten alcohol too. His time came much too soon, and all of us were the worse for it. We are nourished now on the happy memories he has left us, some seventeen years later. His star will shine in the firmament for a long time to come.

Craig Highberger

Jackie hid his hard drug use from many of the friends who loved him and who were not users. I was one of those friends. I spent a lot of time with the calm, sober Jackie, who was extremely funny and witty, highly intelligent—his conversation peppered with cultural references that skewered convention.

In 1985, I lived in Chicago. It had been just a few weeks since I had talked to Curtis. We had home delivery of the *New York Times*. I will never forget how horrible it was to turn the page and see Jackie's obituary.

Paul Ambrose

We all, of course, adored everything and everyone in *The Wizard of Oz*. And Margaret Hamilton lived in New York City, and somehow Jackie got her address from someone who knew her. She said she wanted to send her flowers on her birthday, or something. And, one day, Jackie and Estelle just went over to her building with a bouquet of flowers and told the doorman they had come to see Margaret Hamilton. Of course, the doorman said, "Is Miss Hamilton expecting you?" And Jackie just bold-faced lied and said to him, "Yes, tell Miss Hamilton that Jackie Curtis and his friend Douglas Fisher have flowers for her." And it worked, the doorman called and announced them and sent them on up. They knocked at the door, and there the little old darling was. She was almost eighty years old, and she invited them in and made them tea. Jackie invited her to a party someone was giving, but she declined because she was going to be out of town visiting old friends in Texas. But Jackie stayed in touch with her and called her on the phone, and they exchanged cards and letters for years.

Jackie died on the fifteenth of May 1985, and, coincidentally, Margaret Hamilton died the very next day, May sixteenth. On May seventeenth, the *New York Times* printed both their obituaries. Jackie's was right beside a production still of the Wicked Witch and Dorothy Gale from *The Wizard of Oz*. Curtis would have liked that.

Reverend Timothy Holder

I never felt an ounce of jealousy or resentment from my brother, Jackie. I should maybe say my sister, Jackie, as well. Because I had the father and mother in Tennessee, and all the privileges of an upper-middle-class upbringing: good schools, colleges. And here Jackie was making do on the streets of the Lower East Side. Jackie always loved me very much. So [I reacted] with great sorrow in 1985 when I received a call that he had died of a drug overdose. Just the weekend before, we [had spoken] on the phone, and had planned a reunion of sorts in New York, so he could introduce me to his friends.

My older brother Jackie was a man who was pioneering in areas of sexuality, of gender, and it would be twenty-five years later that I would be sitting at Harvard University in divinity school and the concept of "social construct" [would come] up in class. And we started talking about the fact that the terms "male" and "female" are nothing but constructs by human beings. And we do a lot of labeling and categorizing and stereotyping in society, I think sometimes quite ignorantly and hatefully. I think Jackie knew a lot about who he was, what he was. . . . In his confusion and his pain, and in his struggle, I think there was great truth, and great love.

Sasha McCaffrey

Nobody thought we were going to survive those insane times; nobody really believed that any one of us would live past twenty-five. But I was surprised when Jackie died, because Jackie was not a junkie. I know she hadn't done heroin for a long time. And she had also stopped drinking for a long time. When Jackie did heroin, it was very occasionally. . . . She must have gone back to heroin because she was bored or something. I would never think of my friend Jackie as a heroin addict or a speed freak or an alcoholic. She was an extremely talented person who was struggling with personal problems and doing the best that she could. But she wasn't lucky. I wish she'd know that she was appreciated then—it might have helped.

Rose Royalle

When I cleaned my act up, finally, after going to the limits with drugs and alcohol, I had a counselor I was seeing. This was in 1985, and it was very sad, yet poignant in a way, that this man told me about Jackie's death. I had been in rehab. I didn't know what was going on. And he had been her counselor and found out I knew Curtis, and he said, "Jackie went out on a slip." In other words, she picked up again and died.

I felt very sad that I would never see her again, and also amazed that she had even been in recovery. I think there was some kind of synchronicity there that meant something. It was really significant to me to hear that at that moment in my own recovery process. Actually, I really can't believe that I'm still alive. Obviously, I've been influenced, with all the glitter and hair. I absolutely love Jackie. I loved those times. It makes me really sad that there are so few of us left. But we go on . . .

Penny Arcade

Jackie's death was kind of the last straw in my relationship with Andy Warhol and the Factory. Because Jackie never stopped loving Andy, and Jackie had a very close relationship with Andy—if we can say Andy had close relationships. When Jackie died, I contacted the Factory with the hope that Andy would give Jackie the big Frank Campbell celebrity funeral, like he had given Candy. But at that point, Warhol was making celebrity portraits and commissioned portraits of rich people and politicians. He wanted to distance himself from any drug deaths or any scandal, and he didn't even send flowers.

We gave Jackie an incredible wake, an incredible funeral, and an incredible burial. It was the last great downtown funeral. By the end of the wake, Jackie was completely covered in glitter and had a magic wand under his arm. We stuffed the casket with packs of Kools and photographs of James Dean and Gary Cooper and all kinds of mementos for Jackie; it was a mad, mad, mad wake. Jackie was buried out in the countryside, and at the end of the burial Rita Redd covered Jackie's grave with red glitter. You could see it half a mile away.

Robert Heide

I remember seeing Jackie in his coffin dressed in a man's suit—which was somehow inappropriate. People were putting joints in his jacket pocket, in case Jackie needed to get high in heaven. And the coffin was filled with photographs and glitter and all of the reviews from Jackie's plays. It was a nice send-off.

Jackie Curtis

When I die, I want to be cremated and have my ashes spread all over Greta Garbo's apartment. Seriously, I want a funeral with an open casket. No, I want *two* open caskets: one as Jackie, and one as Curtis.

Paul Ambrose

The wake and funeral were just incredible. Jackie looked like a frog in a tuxedo. He would have appreciated the fact that his face was painted the same color orange that he used to wear on the street. Everybody was just mad at him, sad and angry . . . the nerve of him doing something so stupid. He had warnings, he knew better, and he just wasted his talent, extinguishing his life like that. Everybody appreciated Jackie for his great talent.

Jackie would have approved of the funeral service, which was at the little Catholic church over on Eleventh Street. There was a nice turnout. Many of Jackie's Factory colleagues were there, and a sea of flowers surrounded the casket. But just when you think everything is going to be fine, and they start carrying the casket down the aisle, Jackie's aunt Josie suddenly flings herself onto the casket, sobbing, knocking it out of the pallbearers' hands. Eventually, they picked Josie up and maneuvered the casket out the door. Everyone heads outside, including Penny Arcade and Gomadi—who has had the nerve to show up; none of us could believe it, but there she was—and as they began sliding the casket into the hearse Penny Arcade turned around, glaring at Gomadi, and suddenly started screaming, "Murderer! Murderer!," and just went after her. People actually started running away because you could see Penny was just rabid, and I remember sort of hoping that she would get Gomadi, strangle her with those Gypsy scarves and things. But Gomadi got her own later, as always happens—she overdosed and died later, and nobody missed her.

Jacob Clark

The following diary excerpt is dated May 22, 1985. I wrote it in a Laundromat on Graham Avenue in Williamsburg, Brooklyn:

> Jackie Curtis died last Wednesday of a heroin overdose. I was shocked at first, then resigned and angry. What a fucking waste! I called Jamie Eisenhower and talked to him. He said it was "accidental," but how in the fuck can a heroin OD be accidental? It is voluntarily injected. He told me the pertinent information and on Sunday I went to the funeral home. There were lots of people there—old frayed queens and icons of the downtown underworld. Jamie was out of it, as I imagined he had been since . . .
>
> I viewed Jackie, who appeared stately, almost kingly, in his tux. He looked good except for the pancake makeup slathered over his face. He looked too good and too young to die. It was strange seeing him there—someone had sprinkled glitter over his face. I had just seen him about a month ago at The Bar. He seemed faraway then, perturbed at something. Not at me but at something. He looked around and left as quietly as he had come in. I went to The Bar after the viewing and remembered where he had stood then, and the first time I met him in January 1984. I felt very strange.

The funeral was Monday. At first I wasn't going to go but I did anyway. After all, he was a friend in a very odd and short-lived way. It was Catholic and routine as funerals go. His aunt fainted, there were a lot of tears. At the end, some deranged woman screamed, "I'm going to get you, you fucking bitch!," at another mourner outside the church. I didn't know what started all of that but people said it had something to do with a girl trying to have sex with Jackie as he lay dying. It was an ugly scene.

I stood around and spoke with some of the mourners when it was over and the hearse left for its journey to Westchester. One woman, a crusty, somewhat feisty off-Broadway has-been, fired up a joint and several of us toked. People probably thought we were heathens for smoking dope in front of a church, but somehow, in this case, it seemed appropriate. Everyone wandered off and I went home to change clothes, my mind in a sincere funk.

Holly Woodlawn

One day, I heard that Jackie was dead. I don't like funerals, I don't like coffins, and I will never ever go to another one. I was sitting there during the memorial service, the priest is doing his *Ave Maria* thing, and suddenly the door of the church slams open and this woman is crying hysterically, "I killed him, I killed him," and they dragged this bitch outside. She had been with him when he was shooting heroin and was so guilty about it. I'm going to cry, I know, remembering all of this. They dragged her out and picked up the casket and . . . my friend was gone. I remember going up to the open coffin and seeing Jackie, and that was the last time I ever saw my friend. I couldn't go to the gravesite, where they buried him. I couldn't watch them put his body into the ground. I've had too many friends die on me. Wherever Jackie is, I hope he's happy—because he made me happy.

Ellen Stewart

I am Jackie's family, and we were very close. Jackie always said that I was his mother. When he had bad times, we could always talk about it. He was always very anxious to not do the things that led to his death. He tried very hard. But the world should understand what it is like being an artist, and a very good one. Having an intrinsic belief in yourself—and yet finding it very difficult for the world to believe in you as an artist.

Jackie once said to me that in a way he was doing *Pagliacci*, his version of *Pagliacci*. That is how he felt every time he put lipstick on, pasted on his eyelashes, drew his eyebrows, and selected what wig he was going to wear. How well could he be *Pagliacci* for the coming performance?

Joey Preston

It was very difficult for me, but we had to make sure that Curtis's funeral got off properly. The family could not afford all the burial expenses, and we did not know where the rest of the money was going to come from. But I said a prayer, and through Ellen Stewart and many other kind donations we were able to raise the rest of the money by the end of the funeral. I couldn't have been more moved and happier and more thankful to everyone who had helped.

After the burial, the mound of dirt over Curtis's grave was just embedded with rhinestones and glitter. You could see it for a quarter mile away as we were driving away. I wrote the [inscription for the] tombstone. It says, "Warhol superstar, poet, writer, singer, and actor." Curtis is buried in the same plot with my uncle Jackie, up in Putnam Valley. I go up and visit and put flowers on it all the time, and sit there and reflect.

After Curtis died, it changed my whole outlook about ever getting into the movies, or staying in theater. I enjoyed it, and I thought

I'd have a career out of it, and we all worked together. But when Curtis died, it was suddenly different. It was no longer interesting to me. Curtis was our family star, and he was going to propel us into the universe. When he died, it was a whole world that was lost.

Jackie Curtis Tribute
A poem by Taylor Mead

> Jackie Curtis, Jackie Curtis
> flouncy dame
> sort of.
>
> You're not Jimmie Dean
> you're not Lana Turner.
>
> You were Jackie Curtis
> More individual
> maybe.
>
> You got a wry, bouncy look at life
> and then slipped and fell,
> as only fancy figure skaters
> on pointy heels
> and big city cement ice
> can fall.

Elegy for jackie curtis & his/her hip granma
A poem by Sam Abrams

> we all wanted to be
>   billie holiday
> & we all were
>   some of us discovered

early on
  i'm not gonna be male
  i'm not gonna be female
  i'm not gonna be straight
  i'm not gonna be gay

just gonna be me
containing
all nothing missing &
everything belongs to me
just as good belongs to you
  jackie

you outghta see
all the great clothes
we find in the trash
where we live now

far from bay one
Jackie
You are not truly a Warhol Superstar until you are dead.

GLAMOUR, GLORY AND GOLD: THE LIFE AND LEGEND OF NOLA NOONAN, GODDESS AND STAR

A comedy by
JACKIE CURTIS

Closing monologue of the play. Nola is alone at
her beach house. It is night. A full moon.

NOLA
I like it here. I like the quiet noise, I like the

ocean ... I like the sunset. It's very beautiful. It's not bitter like it was in Chicago. The water ...

(She picks up a seashell)

I had a collection of seashells. My mother threw them down the incinerator. I cried. She told me to shut up, but I wouldn't ... those seashells ... those seashells were the only beautiful things I possessed. I ran away from home. I can't remember how old I was, but I was alone ... without my seashells, my crinolines, my salesman, my iceman ... no one ... that's funny ... I don't remember anything.

(A pause)

Is that you, Mazie? Toulouse ... you're reading a script for me? I can read it myself ... no?

(She looks up.)

Ah, hello moon, hello stars! I'm not up in your sky, but I'm a star! A star!

(A pause)

Arnie, who built this set? It's terribly authentic. Arnie! Arnie, aren't you with us anymore? What? I'm not with you anymore? Then where am I? Where am I, Arnie? If this isn't a set, then where am I?

(There is a long, painful pause)

Somebody answer me! Arnie, I'll be a good girl, I promise ... I'll even finish the picture ... what picture? Where's my speech teacher? Tell her I said "set" ... I said "set" and "get" and "pet" and what ... what ... what?! Oh, just tell her I left all of you saying my "t's" like a pro!

(She begins walking into the ocean)

Ahh, death, escape, escape ... to where? Where?

Where hair has never been hit by the bleach pots...a place where eyelashes remain naked... where lips with that bloodred slash scream out to be kissed, where wrists hang free of gold-plated bracelets that bind you to your studio. Where nails have never known the touch of gleaming polish... perfumed skin, powdered and suffocated in front of inhuman cameras...machines without mercy.

No more necklaces choking...contract signatures, good-bye! Peter...Peter, is that you?

What was I, Peter? What was I? Glamour... glory...golden   girl...admired...idolized... loved...dreamt about, fantasized, publicized, blown up out of proportion on plastic screens all over the world, so some concession stand could sell popcorn in some dingy theater! Looked at, stared at, whistled at, yelled at.

Peter...it's not you, is it, Peter? It never was you!

(The waves are covering her now)

Death...escape clause...escape...ahhh...

(Pause a beat)

What was I?

(Pause a beat)

What was I?

The music comes up, and then out. The lights die.

BLACKOUT

INTERVIEWEE BIOGRAPHIES

PAUL AMBROSE, *actor*

Paul Ambrose first met Jackie Curtis (who was appearing at La Mama in *Cockstrong*) in the late 1960s, shortly after moving to New York City from Tennessee. His first appearance on stage was as Juicy Lucy in Curtis's *Vain Victory*. In 1970, Paul, Jackie, and Candy Darling auditioned in drag for Busby Berkeley for chorus line parts in the Broadway musical revival of *No, No, Nanette*. Unfortunately, none of the three was cast.

MICHAEL ANDRE, *poet, literary editor*

Michael Andre published Jackie Curtis's poem "B-Girls" in *The Poets' Encyclopedia*, a 1979 publication of the literary journal *Unmuzzled Ox*. Jackie's poem is the longest work in the 310-page volume. Andre notes that it is based upon Curtis's observations of the barroom denizens of Slugger Ann's, his grandmother's Lower East Side bar.

ANDREW AMIC-ANGELO, *actor*

Andrew Amic-Angelo played three male leads (Lefty, the one-armed tuba player; mobster Johnny Apollo; and film director Arnie) in the 1974 revival of Jackie Curtis's *Glamour, Glory, and Gold*. He has performed in *Death of a Soldier, A View from the Bridge*, and *Godspell* on Broadway, and in several television series. He lives in Los Angeles.

PENNY ARCADE, *performance artist*

Jackie and Penny met when Penny was in high school, and they shopped thrift stores every weekend looking for 1930s cocktail dresses. Penny appeared in many of Curtis's plays, including *Femme Fatale* and *I Died Yesterday*. She appeared in *Women in Revolt* with Jackie in 1972. Her latest works, including *Bitch!Dyke!Fag-hag! Whore!*, *Bad Reputation*, and *New York Stories*, have toured internationally.

MICHAEL ARIAN, *actor*

Michael Arian first met Jackie Curtis when he joined John Vaccaro's Play-House of the Ridiculous troupe, appearing in Curtis's *Heaven Grand in Amber Orbit*. He partied with Curtis in the back room of Max's Kansas City. Arian lives in New York City and works with Ellen Stewart's La Mama Experimental Theater Club.

GRETCHEN BERG, *photojournalist*

Gretchen Berg met Jackie Curtis in 1965 when she was interviewing and photographing Andy Warhol for *Show* magazine. She took photographs of Jackie for his first portfolio, and they became friends. Berg witnessed Curtis's transformation from an idealistic adolescent boy into the drag persona that brought him fame. She lives in Manhattan.

STYLES CALDWELL, *actor*

Styles Caldwell was a devoted friend of Jackie Curtis's. Curtis lived with Styles in Hollywood in the late seventies while attempting to land the lead role in *The James Dean Story*. In 1983, Styles appeared in *I Died Yesterday* with Curtis.

LEEE BLACK CHILDERS,
ex-manager/promoter for David Bowie, Iggy Pop and the Stooges

Leee Black Childers came to New York in the mid-1960s and met Jackie Curtis at Max's Kansas City. Jackie lived with him off and on, and they were close friends until Leee moved to England in the late seventies. Leee was manager and promoter for various musical artists. He currently is a photographer and writer whose work is featured in the book *PUNK*, a definitive record of a revolution.

JOE DALLESANDRO, *actor*

By 1968, Joe Dallesandro was the toast of the New York underground film scene. The "Little Joe" of Lou Reed's "Walk on the Wild Side" was the enigmatic, often naked star of eight Paul Morrissey films presented by Warhol between 1967 and 1972, including *Flesh* (1968), which costarred Jackie Curtis and Candy Darling. Other films include Francis Coppola's *The Cotton Club* (1984) and *Beefcake* (1999). He lives in West Hollywood.

LAURA DE COPPET, *Author*

Laura de Coppet, a journalist who has contributed to many publications including Andy Warhol's Interview, was an assistant at the John Gibson Gallery during the mid-1970s. She was a close friend and benefactor of Jackie Curtis's. De Coppet was also very close to the late Leo Castelli (Warhol's art dealer), and to Andy himself. She is the author of The Art Dealers.

ALEXIS DEL LAGO, *artist and star*

Alexis del Lago met Jackie Curtis in 1968. Alexis and Jackie were close friends for the next seventeen years, appearing together in many shows and revues. Jackie cast Alexis in a major role in *Americka Cleopatra* in 1970. Alexis's antique shop, The Gilded Lily (1986–2002), was frequented by many Hollywood stars.

HARVEY FIERSTEIN, *Tony Award–winning actor and playwright*

Harvey Fierstein's second appearance on stage in a drag role was in Jackie Curtis's *Americka Cleopatra*. Harvey is an award-winning playwright, actor, and gay rights activist. In 1983, he won Tony Awards for best play and for his starring performance in *Torch Song Trilogy*. One of America's few openly gay major celebrities, Fierstein most recently starred in drag in the hit Broadway musical *Hairspray*.

JOE FRANKLIN, *TV legend*

Jackie Curtis had his first TV exposure on Joe Franklin's *Down Memory Lane*. Franklin began his talk and variety TV show in New York in 1951 and holds the *Guinness Book of World Records* award for hosting the most television shows (31,015). He can be heard today on Bloomberg Radio and WOR-AM in New York.

ROBERT HEIDE, *playwright and author*

Robert Heide met Jackie Curtis through his close friend Ron Link, who directed several of Jackie's plays, including *Glamour, Glory, and Gold*. Heide witnessed Curtis's transformation from a shy young playwright into a powerhouse talent. Heide's plays have been performed at the Caffe Cino, the Judson Church, Cafe La Mama, and Theater for the New City. He is coauthor, with Jon Gilman, of eight books on popular culture in twentieth-century America.

DON HERRON, *photographer, writer, and painter*

Don Herron moved to New York City in the late 1970s, when he began working on a series of portraits of people in their bathtubs, concentrating primarily on performing artists. He currently writes a weekly column for a Hudson Valley newspaper, and divides his time between his East Village apartment (where he photographed Jackie in his own bathtub) and his 1863 town house, sixty miles north on the Hudson River.

REVEREND TIMOTHY HOLDER, *Jackie Curtis's brother*

Reverend Timothy Holder spent summers with his older half brother Jackie Curtis in Tennessee when he was growing up. Today, Holder is an openly gay Episcopal priest.

MELBA LAROSE, JR., *playwright, director, and actress*

Melba LaRose, Jr., starred in the premiere run of Jackie Curtis's *Glamour, Glory, and Gold* in 1967. She also appeared opposite Jackie in *Lucky Wonderful* (1968). As part of her theatrical pursuits, LaRose is also the founder and artistic and administrative director for NY Artists Unlimited, a nonprofit company taking professional theater to underserved audiences.

AGOSTO MACHADO, *actor*

Agosto Machado was a close friend of Jackie Curtis's and appeared in many of Jackie's plays, including *Americka Cleopatra* and *Vain Victory*. Agosto also worked with John Vaccaro's Play-House of the Ridiculous, and on many plays at La Mama. He lives in Manhattan.

SASHA MCCAFFREY, *messenger, personal friend*

In 1966, Sasha McCaffrey was just out of high school and had his first job and his first apartment in the West Village. Holly Woodlawn, Candy Darling, and Jackie Curtis moved in with him, and it was several months before he realized the three were not girls.

TAYLOR MEAD, *poet, actor, superstar*

Warhol superstar Taylor Mead is un-equaled as a pop enigma who's seen it all and done it all. Taylor was in San Francisco in 1956 when the beat poetry scene was getting under way, and he was famous for standing up on bars and screaming his poetry over the noise all the drunks were making. His films for Warhol include *Kiss* (1963), *Tarzan and Jane Regained . . . Sort Of* (1963), *Taylor Mead's Ass* (1964), *Imitation of Christ* (1967), and *Lonesome Cowboys* (1967). Mead continues to write and perform poetry; during 2003, he performed every Friday night at the Bowery Poetry Club in New York City.

SYLVIA MILES, *actress*

Born in Greenwich Village, Sylvia Miles was an Academy Award nominee for her performance as Cass, opposite Jon Voight, in *Midnight Cowboy* (1969). Sylvia was very close to Andy Warhol, and partied with Jackie, Candy Darling, and Holly Wood-lawn. In 1972, she starred in director Paul Morrissey's *Heat*, with Joe Dallesandro. Her most recent roles included appearances in *Sex in the City*, and she has made a big splash as Roxy's trashy mom, Stella, on the ABC soap opera *One Life to Live*.

JACK MITCHELL, *photographer*

Jack Mitchell has earned his living as a photographer since the age of fifteen. After serving in World War II, he spent forty-five years living and working in his studio on New York City's Upper East Side. His photographs have appeared in most national and international publications covering the arts. Mitchell photographed Jackie Curtis and other Warhol superstars extensively during the late sixties and early seventies for *After Dark* magazine, the *New York Times*, and other publications. Curtis is featured in Mitchell's 1998 book of photographs, *Icons & Idols*.

PAUL MORRISSEY, *writer, director*

Paul Morrissey studied literature at Fordham University and began directing independent films in the early 1960s. In 1965, he took charge of operations at the Warhol studio. Morrissey's direction revitalized the films presented by Andy Warhol—from the art house cult classics *Flesh* (1968) and *Women in Revolt* (1972), which starred Jackie Curtis, to his more mainstream successes with *Flesh for Frankenstein* and *Blood for Dracula* (1974). The Cannes Film Festival honored him with an official tribute in 2002.

MICHAEL MUSTO, *entertainment journalist*

Michael Musto is one of the leading entertainment journalists and cultural critics in the United States. Noted for his wit and sardonic humor, he writes the popular *Village Voice* entertainment column "La Dolce Musto," and he contributes to *Interview, Out,* and the *New York Times.* His books include *Downtown* and *Manhattan on the Rocks.* Musto is a regular on E-TV, and his film appearances include *Resident Alien,* a documentary about the life of Quentin Crisp.

JEREMIAH NEWTON, *writer, playwright*

Jeremiah Newton was a beloved friend of Candy Darling's until her death from leukemia in 1974. In 1996, he provided additional scenes and dialogue for the indie hit *I Shot Andy Warhol,* in which Candy is portrayed by Stephen Dorff and Jeremiah is played by Danny Morgenstern. Newton cowrote *My Face for the World to See: The Letters, Diaries and Drawings of Candy Darling, Andy Warhol Superstar,* and recently had a reading from his play *Candy Darling Live and Onstage,* which was part of the 2004 Howl Festival. He is film, television, and video industry liaison for New York University, the largest film school in the world.

JOEY PRESTON, *Jackie Curtis's cousin*

Joey Preston's mother, Josephine, was a featured cast member of Jackie Curtis's *Vain Victory*. As an adolescent, Joey and Jackie sometimes hung out at Slugger Ann's, their grandmother's bar on the Lower East Side. Preston was stage manager and assistant to Curtis for the last six years of his life. He is associate producer of *Superstar in a Housedress*.

RUBY LYNN REYNER

Ruby Lynn Reyner played the title role in Jackie Curtis's smash hit *Heaven Grand in Amber Orbit* at La Mama. Ruby also served as the maid of honor at Jackie's wedding to Eric Emerson. She has been producing and directing her own musicals at La Mama, has produced a CD, *From the Wrong Side of Town*, and is working on her next CD. Her film, shot in the 1970s and featuring Warhol superstars, is finally being completed and will be screened at indie festivals. Ruby remembers Jackie as the only person to make her pee in her panties!

MONA ROBSON, *devoted companion*

Mona Robson met Jackie Curtis in 1965 on Christopher Street when Curtis (in drag) came up to her, saying, "Let's go dancing," by way of introduction. It was the beginning of two decades of friendship. Robson became Curtis's backstage assistant, confidant, and companion.

ROSE ROYALLE, *transgendered entertainer*

As soon as Rose Royalle was old enough to get a drug connection, she ran away to live with bohemians, alcoholics, and street people. She became a close friend of Jackie Curtis's and joined Charles Ludlam's Ridiculous Theater Company. Ludlam cast her as the Turtle Woman in *Turds in Hell* (1969), but, as was her custom, Miss Royalle was too bombed to perform. Today, after rehab, Rose Royalle is one of New York's most popular and influential transgendered performers, noted for her over-the-top outfits.

PAUL SERRATO, *musician and composer*

Paul Serrato met Jackie Curtis in 1967. He composed music for Curtis's *Lucky Wonderful* (1968) and *Vain Victory* (1970). One song from *Vain Victory*, "White Shoulders, Black and Blue," became a cult classic and was Jackie's favorite standard. Serrato acted as musical director for Jackie's 1974 performance in "Cabaret in the Sky." Serrato's recent work includes the highly reviewed jazz CD *More Than Red*.

EDDIE SNYDER, *friend and companion*

Eddie Snyder was one of Jackie Curtis's closest friends and the last person to live with him. He lives in Manhattan and works for the Veterans Administration.

ELLEN STEWART, *founder, La Mama*

Ellen Stewart is founder and director of the La Mama Experimental Theater Club, which began in October 1961. To date, La Mama has presented more than 1,900 productions, and its resident theater troupes have performed throughout the world. Jackie Curtis premiered many of his plays at La Mama, including *Heaven Grand in Amber Orbit*, *Vain Victory*, and his final work, *Champagne* (1985).

LILY TOMLIN, *Tony Award– and Mark Twain Award–winning comedienne*

Hailed as the "New Queen of Comedy" in 1977 on the cover of *Time* magazine, Lily Tomlin is the 2003 winner of the Mark Twain Prize for American Humor. One of America's foremost comedic entertainers, she has enjoyed an extraordinary career spanning all facets of the entertainment industry, including feature films, television, and theater. She made her film debut as Linnea in Robert Altman's *Nashville*, for which she was nominated for an Academy Award, as well as being voted Best Supporting Actress by both the New York Film Critics and the National Society of Film Critics. Lily was a great friend and admirer of Jackie Curtis, and is both the narrator and an interviewee in the film *Superstar in a Housedress*.

JOHN VACCARO, *founder, Play-House of the Ridiculous*

John Vaccaro founded the groundbreaking avant-garde theater company Play-House of the Ridiculous in 1965. Jackie Curtis performed in many works directed by Vaccaro, including *Cockstrong* and *The Life of Lady Godiva*. Vaccaro's troupe performed several of Curtis's plays, including *Heaven Grand in Amber Orbit*, which played at La Mama in 1970 and toured internationally for two years.

STEVEN WATSON, *author*

Steven Watson's most recent work is *Factory Made: Warhol and the Sixties*, published in 2003, which chronicles the lives of Warhol superstars (including Jackie Curtis) and hangers-on. He first met Jackie and began to interview him in the late 1960s. Watson's other works include *Harlem Renaissance* (1996) and *The Birth of the Beat Generation* (1998).

HOLLY WOODLAWN, *superstar*

Actress Holly Woodlawn achieved instant stardom for her performance as a drug addict in *Trash* (1970), a film presented by Andy Warhol and directed by Paul Morrissey. Holly lived with Jackie Curtis, and appeared in the film *Women in Revolt* (1972) and the revue "Cabaret in the Sky" (1974) with Jackie. She has appeared in more than twenty films and television programs. Holly's autobiography, *A Lowlife in High Heels*, was published in 1998.